CONTENTS

ECUADOR TODAY

THOUGH THE REPUBLIC OF ECUADOR IS UNDER TWO HUNDRED years old, the country's history traces back to 10,000 BCE, when pre-Columbian peoples first inhabited the region. Following centuries of conquest, Ecuador ultimately declared independence in 1822 from Spain, their final conqueror. Since achieving independence, the country has seen major political upheaval and sweeping economic changes.

Ecuador is rich in history and natural resources. Many people with differing points of view call Ecuador home. Yet with such diverse geography, inhabitants, and even political ideas, Ecuador tends toward a rapid pace of change that can lead to instability. On the other hand, as a relatively young country, Ecuador embraces change and teems with creativity. The nation is a reminder that all countries must adapt quickly to thrive in today's world.

The Pastaza River zigzags through the Amazon jungle.

RESOURCES, RICHES, AND STRIFE

Ecuador's geography is as diverse as its culture. The country is divided into four regions, and each region has unique features. From the jungles of the Oriente to the biodiversity of the Galápagos Islands and the volcanoes of the Sierra, Ecuador packs a range of landscapes into a relatively small space— the country is a bit smaller than the state of Nevada.

Much of the country's character, history, and economy has been shaped by its geography. Ecuador's natural resources, including petroleum reserves, are a major part of the nation's revenue. Petroleum is so important to the Ecuadorian economy that it brings in over half of the country's export income. Balancing Ecuador's bottom line with the preservation of the environment has caused tension, both within the country and internationally.

President Rafael Correa came up with an unprecedented tactic in 2007 when he announced that Ecuador would "auction" the Yasuni rain forest to avoid drilling for oil there. Correa's plan was that countries with more robust economies could pledge money, which would offset the lost revenue from not drilling. Correa's solution drew both praise and criticism. In 2013, after raising only $129 million US dollars (USD) out of the $7.2 billion USD he had set out to collect, President Correa scrapped the plan. The government has begun to issue drilling permits. The many indigenous peoples who inhabit Ecuador (and live in areas that to this point have not been developed or affected by drilling) believe that Correa has not done enough to stand up for the environment. For his part, President Correa believes he's made major strides toward preservation despite the failure of the Yasuni auction. Ecuador is the first nation in the world to include the rights of nature in its constitution, a constitution spearheaded by Correa's administration in 2008.

President Rafael Correa at a national military parade in Quito in 2012.

RAFAEL CORREA: THE FACE OF ECUADOR

Rafael Correa's presidency has been representative of the constant tide of change in Ecuador. Even his predecessors show the political instability in the nation: Correa succeeded Alfredo Palacio as president. Palacio, who had been vice president under Lucio Gutiérrez, was named president after Gutiérrez was removed from office by Congress. Correa has earned widespread support of voters. His approval rating hovers at 50 percent or higher. Correa spends a sizable amount of oil revenue on social programs that help the Ecuadorian people. Yet Correa's administration has been plagued by problems that could change the way Ecuador is governed.

One major criticism of Correa is that he has limited free speech in Ecuador. Correa has issued executive orders that allow his government to shut down organizations that are critical of Correa's policies. Documented instances of

Historically, the Shuar people have worn brightly colored clothes and tattoos.

Correa's hold on the media include fining newspapers for running critical political cartoons, jailing journalists, limiting the travel of journalists, and censorship.

Correa's decisions impact more than the citizens in Ecuador. In 2008, Ecuador decided to default on its foreign debt, which President Correa labeled "illegitimate." The unpaid debt totaled more than $3 billion USD. The default affected foreign markets, as well as Ecuador's. The country has since reentered international markets but is considered a high-risk investment.

THE FIRST ECUADORIANS

Aside from its natural beauty and fast-paced political system, Ecuador is known for the diversity of its population. Up to four million Ecuadorians are indigenous peoples. They hail from native cultures such as the Shuar, Kichwa, and Awa. Native Americans populated Ecuador for centuries before the Spanish arrived to colonize the country. As such long-living cultures, the indigenous people of Ecuador have their own languages, customs, and lifestyles. Some cultures still live off of the land in remote areas of the rain forest, while others embrace their cultures as a facet of their lives in more developed cities and towns. Maintaining an ancient culture in Ecuador can be very difficult. Not only are many groups fighting to preserve their way of life, but the indigenous people of Ecuador often face disproportionate poverty.

As a means of securing rights, in 1986 a group of indigenous people formed the Confederation of Indigenous Nationalities of Ecuador (CONAIE). The organization is a way for indigenous people of different nationalities to come

together to advocate for education, medical care, and land rights, among other issues. The group has largely succeeded in making sure its voice is heard. At times, this involves disruptive tactics like large-scale protests that bring regular daily life in cities around Ecuador to a halt. CONAIE demonstrates that in a country as varied as Ecuador, there are often competing interests.

Guayaquil's colorful houses capture the city's liveliness.

CELEBRATING DIFFERENCE

Ecuador's diversity might cause tension at times, but it is also the nation's greatest strength. Ecuador benefits from the unique perspectives of its citizens. The country offers something for everyone: from coastal towns to its bustling capital city; industry to indigenous life; and exciting food, music, and sports. As Ecuador navigates political change and develops its economy, the country is increasingly one to watch.

GEOGRAPHY

Machalilla National Park is just one of Ecuador's eleven national parks.

1

ECUADOR IS LOCATED IN WESTERN South America, where it borders Colombia and Peru. The country's 15.8 million citizens share 109,483 square miles (283,561 square kilometers) of territory. While many Ecuadorians also share cultural similarities, Ecuador's geography results in varied ways of life for its people. Those living in the capital city of Quito have a very different experience from the indigenous peoples living in the Amazon, for example. Ecuador's geography is stunningly diverse; it includes volcanoes, beaches, mountains (including the world-famous Mount Chimborazo), rivers, and plains. The nation's geography sustains an impressive array of plants and animals, too.

THE FOUR REGIONS

Differences in altitude between the various regions account for the great diversity of climates in Ecuador.

Ecuador has twenty-four provinces.

THE SIERRA Two major chains of the Andes Mountains, running from north to south, form the Sierra: the Cordillera Occidental and the Cordillera Oriental. The Cordillera Oriental is wider, and its peaks average over 13,100 feet (4,000 meters) in altitude. The Cordillera Occidental, however, includes the highest point in Ecuador, Mount Chimborazo, at 20,556 feet (6,265 m).

The Andes Mountains include numerous volcanoes and peaks that rise to more than 20,000 feet (6,096 m). While the southern Sierra is an area of ancient volcanism (where volcanoes have eroded into lower peaks), the northern Sierra constitutes an area of modern volcanism: its volcanoes stand higher and were formed more recently.

The Sierra includes over thirty peaks of volcanic origin, several of which are still active. The region is often subjected to powerful geological forces, such as earthquakes and tremors. The Sierra used to be the most densely populated region of Ecuador, although melting snowcaps from the volcanoes could wreak havoc on inhabitants of the Sierra by burying homes in mudslides and avalanches. By 1947, the Costa's population density had surpassed that of the Sierra.

Between the Cordilleras lies a plateau rich with volcanic soil. Several mountain spurs, called *nudos* (NOO-dohs), cut across the plateau, defining large, isolated basins between the Cordilleras.

The most active volcano in Ecuador is Sangay, with an elevation of 17,158 feet (5,230 m). Sangay has been almost constantly active throughout recorded history, but it is located far from major urban centers so it poses no immediate threat to people.

Beaches meet the city in the Costa region.

THE COSTA The coastal region of Ecuador consists of coastal lowlands, coastal mountains, and rolling hills separating river valleys. The widest part of the region is only 93 miles (150 km) wide, from the coast of Manabí Province to the foothills of the Andes. The narrowest part, in the southern area of Guayas Province, measures 10 miles (16 km) in width.

A coastal mountain chain, the Cordillera Costañera, which extends from Esmeraldas in the north to Guayaquil in the south, divides the Costa into the Costa Externa and the Costa Interna. The lowlands of the Costa Externa lie closest to the coast, while the Costa Interna lies next to the Andes. The coastal lowlands do not exceed 650 feet (198 m) in elevation; even the coastal mountains rise to less than 3,300 feet (1,006 m).

THE ORIENTE After a severe drought in the Sierra in the 1950s, the government encouraged people to colonize the jungle frontier, previously inhabited only by isolated indigenous groups. Given incentives such as tax exemptions for businesses and land deeds for migrants, thousands of

The San Rafael Falls is the largest waterfall in Ecuador.

homesteaders migrated to the Oriente, arriving from Colombia and parts of Ecuador in droves.

The discovery and exploitation of oil reserves in northeastern Ecuador in 1967 and the rapid colonization of the Oriente have distressed the environment and its indigenous inhabitants enormously, forcing many of the reclusive indigenous Amazonians to retreat farther into the forest.

THE GALÁPAGOS ISLANDS Ecuador claimed possession of the Galápagos Islands, officially known as the Archipiélago de Colón, in 1832. Named for the giant tortoises that inhabit the islands, the archipelago consists of nineteen islands and several islets. The entire landmass of the Galápagos is 3,093 square miles (8,010 sq km), located about 600 miles (965 km) west of the coast of Ecuador. At 75 miles (120 km) long, the largest island, Isabela, constitutes more than half of that area. It also contains the islands' highest point, Volcán Wolf, at 5,600 feet (1,707 m).

WEATHER CONDITIONS

The Costa experiences seasonal variations in temperature. It tends to be cooler during the dry season and hotter during the rainy season, especially February through April. The average coastal temperatures range from 73 degrees Fahrenheit (22.5 degrees Celsius) in the south to 79°F (26°C) in the north. There is little seasonal variation except when the El Niño phenomenon causes drastic changes in the climate. The Costa Interna is separated from the effects of ocean currents by the Cordillera Costañera. The climate tends to be hot and humid, with temperatures averaging 79°F (26°C). The rainy season, or winter, lasts from December through May, and is characterized by constant rainfall.

The climate of the Sierra tends to depend more on altitude than on seasonal change. The hottest month averages about 61°F (16°C), and the coolest month drops to about 55°F (12.6°C). Temperatures vary more through the course of the day, in fact, due to the strong sunshine and the high altitude. Mornings are often bright and sunny; the afternoons are cloudy, often with heavy downpours of rain; and the evenings can be chilly and blanketed in thick fog. The residents of Quito like to note that one can experience "all of the seasons in one day" in the capital city.

The relatively uniform climate of the Oriente varies only slightly between the two subregions. The eastern lowlands exemplify an equatorial climate with abundant rainfall, which sometimes measures nearly 200 inches (508 cm) in a year. Temperatures average 77°F (25°C) in the western portion. The jungle of the Oriente also receives high levels of rainfall and average temperatures higher than 82°F (27.5°C).

PLANTS AND WILDLIFE

Due to the great variety of habitats within its small territory, ecologists consider Ecuador one of the most species-rich countries in the world. Well over twenty thousand plant species have been recorded in Ecuador, and new

El Niño is a climatological phenomenon that occurs at irregular intervals every six or seven years. Due to a change in atmospheric pressure, the warm ocean currents that normally flow from January through April instead flow for a longer period, raising temperatures, ocean tides, and humidity. Ocean temperatures increase so much that a lot of marine life is unable to survive. El Niño damages the food supply at the lower end of the food chain, affecting many other species, including marine iguanas and seabirds. It can also cause flooding and landslides. El Niño was particularly harsh between 1982 and 1983, when it caused severe problems for the fishing industry, as well as for Galápagos marine life.

The name El Niño means "baby boy" and is a reference to the baby Jesus and to the fact that the current usually arrives around Christmas.

species are discovered every year. In comparison, the entire continent of North America holds about twenty thousand species.

FLORA AND FAUNA OF THE GALÁPAGOS Bird species populate the island most visibly. There are fifty-six native bird species on the Galápagos, plus about thirty migrant species. Of the native species, forty-five are endemic, meaning that they do not breed anywhere else in the world. The most well-known Galápagos birds include the blue-footed booby, the Galápagos penguin (the most northerly penguin in the world), the red-footed booby, frigate birds (which have a spectacular courtship display), flamingos, and, of course, Darwin's finches.

Mammals had a harder time migrating to the Galápagos because of the distance. Only six mammal species are endemic to the islands: seals, bats, sea lions, dolphins, whales, and rice rats. Other mammals include feral goats, pigs, burros, cats, dogs, and mice. Relatively few small land mammals and insects inhabit the islands, but larger land mammals are common because settlers brought their domesticated livestock with them. People inhabit only five of the islands, constituting a population of more than twenty-five thousand (2010). This figure is rapidly rising as people continue to come from the mainland in search of employment. Residents of the Galápagos make a living primarily from tourism, fishing, and farming. More than half of them live in the city of Puerto Ayora on Isla Santa Cruz, the second-largest island.

Twenty-two reptile species inhabit the islands, nineteen of which are endemic. These include Galápagos tortoises, marine turtles, the ubiquitous iguanas and lizards, geckos, and three species of snakes, all of which are nonpoisonous constrictors.

Galápagos waters contain more than 307 species of tropical fish, at least 50 of which are native. In addition to parrotfish, angelfish, and pufferfish, there are several species of sharks and rays. Many invertebrates populate the waters and beaches, including crabs, sponges, octopuses, starfish, sea urchins, and sea cucumbers.

Galápagos tortoises can live upward of one hundred years in the wild.

Mangrove trees (pictured here) are protected at the Cuyabeno Nature Reserve.

Approximately 1,300 species of plants have been recorded in the Galápagos. They are spread out among six different zones of vegetation. These vary on the larger islands from arid desert to lush tropical highland vegetation.

THE COSTA The cold Peruvian Current, which cools Ecuador's coastal waters, is the primary influence on the climate of the Costa and thus on its flora. The northern corner of Esmeraldas and the southeastern corner of the Costa consist of tropical rain forest. Flora in this area includes trees, lianas (climbing vines), and epiphytes, which are plants that take all of their moisture and some of their nutrients from the humid air. In the Guayas River valley, the forest contains balsa, which is exploited for use as a light lumber.

The vegetation between Esmeraldas and the Gulf of Guayaquil is characterized by dry forests of deciduous and semideciduous trees, which lose their leaves during the dry season.

Thick mangrove forests once covered the swampy coast and the river floodplains. Most of the mangroves, however, have been cleared away for the farming of shrimp—thus endangering the breeding grounds of many animal species.

THE SIERRA Most of the native highland vegetation has been replaced by agricultural crops or altered by periodic burning. The valleys are covered with thorny woodlands, which change to low evergreen forests at the edges. Tropical cloud forests are found at higher elevations in the more isolated valleys. In these rare environments, trapped clouds drench the forest with a fine mist, nourishing a variety of plants, such as ferns, orchids, and other epiphytes, and such rare animals as the woolly tapir, the Andean spectacled bear, and the puma.

The highland area above 11,500 feet (3,500 m) is known as the *páramo* (PAHR-ah-moh); its bleak environment supports little more than hard bunchgrasses and small herbaceous plants. Ecuador's national bird, the Andean condor, makes its home in the páramo and has a wingspan of nearly 10 feet (3 m).

THE ORIENTE The Oriente consists primarily of tropical rain forest with vegetation similar to the Costa. A wide variety of monkeys inhabit the rain forest, as well as sloths, jaguars, ocelots, and smaller carnivores. The rain forest also contains several hoofed animals, including the tapir, deer, and peccary (a relative of the pig, covered with long, dark bristles). Many of these mammals serve as a source of food for Oriente peoples.

A wide variety of parrots and toucans also populate the rain forest, as does the large harpy eagle, which is capable of snatching monkeys and sloths off trees as it flies by. Approximately one thousand species of fish have been recorded, including the electric eel and the piranha.

Ecuador has a stunning variety of amphibians and reptiles. Some of the more exotic frogs include marsupial frogs, who carry their eggs and hatched tadpoles in pouches under their skin, and poison dart frogs, whose skin glands exude toxins strong enough to cause paralysis and death in animals and humans. Indigenous people who are forest dwellers use these toxins as a poison for the tips of their hunting arrows.

RIVERS

Ecuador's rivers generally rise in the Sierra and flow either east toward the Amazon or west toward the Pacific Ocean. They originate either from melted snow at the edges of the mountain snowcaps or from the heavy rains that occur at higher elevations.

Two major river systems drain the Costa: the Guayas and the Esmeraldas. Nearly 40 miles (64 km) in length, the Guayas River forms at the juncture of the Daule and Babahoyo Rivers. The Esmeraldas River system originates in the Sierra as the Guayllabamba River. It flows west out of the Sierra for

"Because the Earth is not a perfect sphere and has an equatorial bulge, the highest point on the planet furthest from its center is Mount Chimborazo not Mount Everest, which is merely the highest peak above sea level." –CIA World Factbook

Quito's colonial architecture draws nearly a million tourists each year.

nearly 200 miles (320 km), emptying into the Pacific Ocean near the town of Esmeraldas.

The major rivers of the Oriente include the Pastaza, the Napo, and the Putumayo. The Pastaza is formed by the confluence of the Chambo and Petate Rivers, which flow out of the Sierra. The Pastaza includes the 200-foot (61 m) Agoyán waterfall. The Napo River rises near Mount Cotopaxi and ranges in width from 1,640 feet (500 m) to well over 1 mile (1.6 km) wide. The Napo is the primary river used for transportation in the eastern lowlands. The Putumayo forms part of the border with Colombia.

URBAN LIVING

Nearly 65 percent of all Ecuadorians live in cities. Regional rivalries are intense between the Sierra and the Costa, and animosities center on the respective regional urban centers, Quito and Guayaquil. While Quito is the center of government, Guayaquil is Ecuador's largest city and main port. The rivalry between the two cities dates back to colonial times, and even today, there is an unspoken rule that if the president is a Quiteño, then the vice president should be a Guayaquileño, and vice versa.

QUITO Ecuador's capital is the second-largest city, with a population of almost 1.73 million in 2015. Quito is located in the northern part of the Sierra, and the site has been inhabited since pre-Columbian times. It is a very old and beautiful city, with a mixture of colonial and modern architecture. In 1978, UNESCO (short for the United Nations Educational, Scientific and Cultural Organization) declared Quito's colonial center, with its old plazas and churches, to be one of the world's cultural heritage sites.

GUAYAQUIL Guayaquil is the most populous city, with over 2.7 million people in 2015, and the economic center of Ecuador. Guayaquileños live in crowded, hot, and humid conditions, yet they pride themselves on their easy-going lifestyle and their irreverent sense of humor. People seem to respond to the heat with accelerated gaiety, and the streets are in constant motion with cars, taxis, buses, street vendors, and pedestrians.

The city is overcrowded and continues to grow as farmers and agricultural workers from the countryside migrate to look for work in the urban areas. The rural-urban migration has led to the formation of large shantytowns, which generally have no electricity or sewage facilities.

Guayaquil is the capital city of Guayas Province, which takes its name from Guayas, the chief of the Punás. Legend says that he courageously resisted conquest by both the Incas and the Spaniards. He killed his wife, Quill, before drowning himself in order to prevent the Spaniards from capturing them. Guayaquil is named after the couple.

INTERNET LINKS

www.cia.gov/library/publications/the-world-factbook/geos/ec.html
The CIA's official website provides maps, photos, and details about Ecuador's terrain.

travel.nationalgeographic.com/travel/countries/ecuador-facts
National Geographic's guide to Ecuador describes the nation's four regions.

www.quito.com.ec/en
The city of Quito's official site consists of everything from an overview of the city to suggested accommodations and cultural events.

HISTORY

The Temple of the Sun in Ingapirca is Ecuador's most important Inca site.

2

ECUADOR'S HISTORY BEGINS WELL before the pre-Columbian empires that once reigned over large swaths of South America. These empires, most notably the Inca Empire, were decimated when Europeans arrived in the sixteenth century. It would be nearly three hundred years before Ecuadorians claimed independence from foreign rulers.

Archaeologists have discovered in Ecuador the most ancient ceramic artifacts of all of the Americas. The oldest ceramics, dating back to 3500 BCE, belong to the Valdivia culture (4800-1200 BCE), which flourished along the coast, near the present-day province of Manabí.

This terra-cotta figure is a Valdivia artifact.

The Inca civilization produced artists with amazing skill.

As Ecuadorians charted the course of their nation, political turnover became the norm. The fledgling nation saw coups and radical, disruptive protests. Contemporary Ecuadorian history has continued this trend. Changing governments, significant oil reserves, and the increasing political participation of everyday people all combine to make history in modern-day Ecuador.

PRE-COLUMBIAN HISTORY

The Inca civilization was the most advanced civilization in pre-Columbian South America. Inca culture and society were organized as a hierarchy headed by the Sapa Inca, who was their god in human form. The Inca Empire, called Tawantinsuyu in the language of the indigenous people, was centered in modern-day Peru but extended into Chile, Bolivia, and Ecuador. In the 1450s, the Inca Empire began its expansion northward into present-day Ecuador, finally conquering the Shyris around modern Quito in 1463.

The empire peaked during the reign of the eleventh Sapa Inca, Huayna Cápac. He ruled through the local chiefs as long as they were willing to accept the divine authority of the Sapa Inca and pay tribute to the empire. If he met any resistance, he would send large groups of the local population to distant areas of the Inca Empire, replacing them with colonists from as far away as modern-day Bolivia and Chile. The Salasaca and Saraguro indigenous tribes of present-day Ecuador are descendants of such relocated Inca colonists.

THE END OF AN EMPIRE

The death of Huayna Cápac by an unknown disease (possibly carried by the Europeans, who were already making their way south from Mexico) sparked a civil war between his two sons, Atahualpa and Huáscar. Huáscar was defeated by Atahualpa only days before the Spaniards arrived in Ecuador.

Ancient Ecuadorian history is referred to as the pre-Columbian period. Christopher Columbus's discovery of the "New World" in 1492 is the dividing line that separates the history of early South American peoples from the region's contemporary history. The arrival of Christopher Columbus in the Americas set off an era of exploration that resulted in an age of conquest.

Historians have many unanswered questions about life in Ecuador's pre-Columbian civilizations. Some scholars point to the climate of Ecuador as the reason: the humidity of the tropics isn't conducive to the preservation of artifacts.

Francisco Pizarro was one of many adventurers who joined the conquest of South America seeking riches for Spain and especially for himself. Pizarro landed on the coast of Ecuador in 1531 but waited until September 24, 1532, to march south. He encountered Atahualpa, the new Sapa Inca, almost by coincidence. Atahualpa was resting near Cajamarca, following the defeat and

This print depicts Pizarro's encounter with Atahualpa.

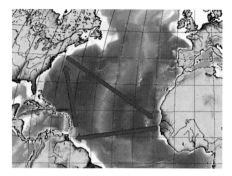

The "Triangular Trade" of rum, slaves, and sugar.

capture of his brother Huáscar. He had known of the arrival of the Europeans for months but did not feel threatened by them. Perhaps he was so secure in his own invincible divinity as the Sapa Inca that he felt no fear; or perhaps he assumed that his forces, which far outnumbered Pizarro's, could easily defeat the Europeans.

Pizarro summoned Atahualpa for a meeting. Atahualpa responded in the company of several thousand of his best troops. The Spanish chaplain who accompanied Pizarro called upon Atahualpa to submit to the Spanish crown and to the Christian god. Atahualpa threw the Bible he was given to the ground, at which point concealed Spanish soldiers opened fire. They killed thousands in the ambush and took Atahualpa captive on November 16, 1532.

Pizarro held Atahualpa in prison for several months. Atahualpa offered a ransom for his life—a room full of gold and two rooms full of silver. Despite a promise to free Atahualpa upon receiving the ransom, Pizarro ordered him to be hanged on August 29, 1533.

SPANISH DOMINION

Ecuador's indigenous population at the time of the conquest was somewhere between 750,000 and 1 million. The Natives were forced to work as laborers. They had few rights and little protection from abuse. The Spaniards gathered tribute from the Inca subjects in the form of goods and labor. They also brought new diseases, to which the Incas had no immunity.

Spanish oppression of the Natives led to unrest and upheaval in the colonies. Rebellions against the Spaniards erupted throughout the entire colonial period. The first major rebellion broke out in 1780, led by Tupac Amaru II, who claimed direct descent from the Sapa Inca. The rebellion gained a large following among the rural people but not among the townspeople, and it was soon put down. The Spaniards captured and killed not only Tupac Amaru, but also his children and many of his relatives.

African slaves were expensive compared to the nearly free labor of indebted Natives, who were called Indians. However, African slaves were accustomed to working in the hot, humid conditions of the coastal plantations, whereas highland peoples could not tolerate the heat. By the end of the colonial period, approximately sixty thousand people of African descent lived in Ecuador.

INDEPENDENCE

In 1808, Napoleon Bonaparte placed his brother Joseph on the Spanish throne. Spanish citizens living in Ecuador resented this and organized local action groups loyal to the Spanish king, Ferdinand VII. In October 1820, a local junta declared independence in Guayaquil, led by the poet José Joaquín Olmedo. The rebels appealed to independence movements in Venezuela and Argentina. Both countries responded promptly with troops.

Simón Bolívar
(1783-1830)

In 1822, two months after the Battle of Pichincha, rebel leader Simón Bolívar entered Quito with a hero's welcome. Ecuador joined the Confederation of Gran Colombia, which included present-day Venezuela and Colombia. For the next several years, Ecuador, as the District of the South, was on the frontlines of a war against Spanish forces in Peru. Growing separatist tendencies within the confederation finally persuaded Ecuadorian leaders in Quito to dissolve their union with Gran Colombia in May 1830. The first name of the new country was El Estado del Ecuador en Colombia. By August, a constituent assembly had drawn up a constitution for the new country, which they named the Republic of Ecuador.

DEMOCRATIC VOICES

The new country was plagued by political instability as the political elite fought among themselves through the first thirty years of independence. Between 1830 and 1925, the country was governed by forty different regimes.

José María Velasco Ibarra served as Ecuador's president five times before he was overthrown for the fourth and final time in 1972.

Between 1830 and 1860, liberal and conservative strongmen vied for control through unconstitutional seizures of power.

The rivalry between Quito and Guayaquil, which was to characterize Ecuadorian politics for at least the next 150 years, was becoming more pronounced. Quito was the home of the politically and religiously conservative landed elite, who resisted change and depended on the indigenous labor force to work their large estates. Guayaquil had developed into a cosmopolitan, bustling seaport whose liberal residents supported free enterprise and anticlericalism.

From 1860 to 1895, the conservatives controlled the government, most notably through Gabriel García Moreno, who ruled the country from 1860 to 1875. The Liberal Party ruled the country from 1895 to 1925. José Eloy Alfaro was party leader until 1912, when he was killed by a mob instigated by his party rival, Leonidas Plaza Gutiérrez. The period from 1925 to 1948 was marked by economic crisis, political instability, and civil unrest. A total of twenty-two heads of state governed the country during this period, and only one successfully completed his term.

The recent history of Ecuador is tied to the discovery of its most important resource—oil—in 1967. One of the reasons that the military took power from 1972 to 1979 was to maintain national ownership of the oil. During this time, the promise of riches from oil inspired massive international borrowing. The loans funded development in the country but left Ecuador vulnerable to the demands of international financial institutions when the debts came due in the 1980s and 1990s.

The instability that has plagued elected governments in the last several decades results from the fact that the Ecuadorian poor, middle-class, and indigenous populations will not tolerate more economic hardship to pay foreign debts. Ecuador's indigenous peoples have found their voice and power in recent years. At around 30 percent of the population, they constitute a sizeable minority that has come to represent the political will of all poor and even some middle-class nonindigenous Ecuadorians.

Popular protest has become a powerful weapon and continues to topple unresponsive governments. President Jamil Mahuad was forced from office in 2000 by a popular uprising that included Colonel Lucio Gutiérrez.

Gutiérrez was elected president in 2002 but was ousted in 2005 for corruption and for failing to fulfill his promises to the poor. His vice president, Alfredo Palacio, held office until 2006, when Rafael Correa—the current president—was elected. Correa has not been immune from the upheaval that preceded him. Correa faced an unsuccessful coup attempt in 2010.

Farmers protest against Jamil Mahuad in 2000.

INTERNET LINKS

www.britannica.com/place/Ecuador
The *Encyclopedia Britannica* hosts a comprehensive entry about the history of Ecuador.

www.history.com/topics/inca
Find articles, videos, and photo galleries about the Inca on this History Channel website.

whc.unesco.org/en/statesparties/ec
Learn about the history of Ecuador through the nation's preserved historical sites on UNESCO's official page.

GOVERNMENT

Carondelet Palace is the seat of the Ecuadorian government.

3

SINCE ACHIEVING COMPLETE independence in 1830, Ecuador has ratified twenty constitutions. The latest incarnation of the constitution was adopted in 2008, with a referendum in 2011 bringing additional changes. The nation has also had eight presidents in the last eighteen years, in spite of the fact that each was elected for a four-year term. These numbers are indicative of the rapid political changes that have characterized Ecuador since it became a republic. Today, many Ecuadorian special interest groups make their voices heard not just through voting but also through protests.

EXECUTIVE BRANCH

The president is both chief of state and head of government. As of now, the president is elected to a four-year term and can be re-elected once.

The executive branch includes the president, the vice president, and a cabinet of ministers. Cabinet positions include ministers of agriculture, culture, environment, national defense, urban development and housing,

Ecuador is a democratic state headed by a president. All Ecuadorians between the ages of eighteen and sixty-five are required to vote unless they are disabled or sick, absent from the country, or otherwise incapacitated. They must directly elect the president and vice president by an absolute majority, which usually requires a second round of elections.

economic and social inclusion, education, electricity and renewable energy, mines, public health, labor relations, and tourism, among others. There are twenty-nine ministers in all. In addition, there are two secretaries, the national secretary of planning and development and the secretary general of public administration.

LEGISLATIVE BRANCH

The Ecuadorian National Assembly (also called Congress) is elected at the same time as the president, every four years. Representatives, called assembly persons, are selected by province, and the assembly is based in Quito. There are 137 seats in the assembly.

An Ecuadorian citizen casts his ballot in the 2013 presidential election.

AN ENDLESS PRESIDENCY?

Ecuador's current constitution sets the strict presidential two-term limit outlined above. Yet President Correa—who was elected in 2007—is already serving his third term in office, despite the two-term limit. Correa ran for reelection in 2009, shortly after the new constitution took effect. Correa's easy victory in that election counts as his first term in office because it's the first term he served under the new constitution. Correa's second term ends in 2017, but critics worry that he'll seek reelection anyway.

President Correa is looking into changing the constitution to end presidential term limits. So far the Ecuadorian Constitutional Court has approved the change. Now Congress will have its turn to vote. These legal maneuvers have led many to compare Correa to Venezuelan president Hugo Chavez, who held office from 1999 until his death in 2013.

According to the constitution:

The National Assembly shall be comprised of:
1. Fifteen (15) Assembly persons elected as representatives of the nation as a whole (national district).
2. Two (2) Assembly persons elected for each province, plus one (1) additional Assembly person for every two hundred thousand (200,000) inhabitants or fraction thereof over one hundred fifty thousand (150,000), on the basis of the last national population census.
3. The law shall determine the election of Assembly persons representing regions, metropolitan districts, and the district representing Ecuadorians living abroad.

The National Assembly passes laws, decides on taxes, and approves international treaties and the annual budget composed by the executive branch. The president can veto congressional decisions. Prior to the 2008 constitution, the legislative body of Ecuador was the National Congress.

JUDICIAL BRANCH

The National Court of Justice and the Constitutional Court are the highest courts in the country. There are also provincial courts, tribunals, special courts to hear election disputes, and cantonal courts, which are courts for different territories within provinces.

In an attempt to correct for corruption and poor training among judges, the Judiciary Council was created in 2008. Nine members presided over this body until 2011. Their mandate was to investigate complaints of improper

The National Court of Justice in Quito is one of the two most important courts in the country.

Ecuador's relationship with the United States and Europe is often described as "rocky" or "strained." Though the US is a major trade partner of Ecuador, the two nations disagree on important policy points. Some of the biggest disagreements relate to Ecuador's offers of political asylum. The government of Ecuador offered asylum to Julian Assange in 2012.

Assange, the founder of WikiLeaks, is wanted in Sweden on criminal charges. After posting bail, Assange took refuge in Ecuador's London embassy and received asylum there. He has been living in the embassy ever since.

Ecuador also offered asylum to Edward Snowden (right) in 2013. Snowden, like Assange, leaked US intelligence. While Snowden did not ultimately accept Ecuador's offer of political asylum, an Ecuadorian official helped arrange Snowden's travel plans from Hong Kong (where he initially fled) to Russia, where he now lives.

procedure by judges and court staff. The council was created as a response to widespread distrust of the impartiality of the judicial system. A referendum to the constitution in 2011 disbanded the Judiciary Council in favor of the Transitional Judiciary Council, which lasted until 2013. While in power, the Transitional Judiciary Council had the power to hire and fire judges at all levels of the judicial branch. President Correa stated that the Transitional Judiciary Council was able to fight corruption better than its predecessor. The new council that replaced the Transitional Judiciary Council, however, has raised some questions. Correa's critics believe that the new council is another way for Correa to expand his power in the judicial branch.

THE ROLE OF THE MILITARY

The military establishment has historically played an important role, directly or indirectly, in Ecuadorian politics. The Ecuadorian military identified itself not with the elite, landowning class but with the merchant class. The military has historically viewed itself as an agent of progressive change.

However progressive and mild the military dictators of Ecuador have been, they nonetheless governed unconstitutionally, from their seizure of power to their abuse of human rights. Although the 1979 constitution defines the armed forces as nonpolitical and as an instrument of civil authority, the

Ecuador's embassy in London, England.

military continues to exert an influence over the political process. After the 1979 transition to democracy, the military prohibited any investigation into human rights issues by President Jaime Roldós.

POLITICAL PARTIES

Ecuador has so many political parties that it is difficult to keep all the acronyms straight. In addition, many deputies run as independents. Some parties are affiliated with particular ideological platforms, such as the Marxist-Leninists, while others are considered the legacies of particular political personalities, such as the Roldistas, who adhere to the ideas of former president Jaime Roldós, who was killed in suspicious circumstances in 1981. Still others, such as Pachakutik, are affiliated with ethnic elements. Pachakutik is the party representing indigenous political goals. All told, there are more than twenty different party organizations competing for power in Ecuador. The Alianza PAIS Party currently holds the most seats (one hundred) in Congress.

INTERNET LINKS

www.economist.com/topics/ecuador
The *Economist*'s site features a roundup of articles about politics in Ecuador.

www.ecuador.org/nuevosite/index_e.php
The page of the embassy of Ecuador includes up-to-date information about industry, culture, travel, and breaking news.

globaledge.msu.edu/countries/ecuador/government
Michigan State University's "Global Insights" summarizes the structure of Ecuador's government, outlines election cycles, and provides a synopsis of international relations.

www.presidencia.gob.ec
The official website of the President of Ecuador (in Spanish).

ECONOMY

E CUADOR'S NATURAL RESOURCES have been the driving force of its economy since the country first started exporting cocoa in the 1800s. Today, Ecuador's economy relies heavily on another resource: oil. Ecuador's oil reserves are concentrated mostly in the Oriente. The republic privatized the oil industry in 2010. Much of the money earned from drilling is used to fund social programs to alleviate poverty; around 60 percent of Ecuadorians live at or below the poverty line.

Ecuador's other exports include textiles, wood products, and chemicals. The country's beauty and exciting landscape draws in tourists from around the world. Tourism accounted for $1.2 billion in revenue in 2013.

LIVING OFF OF THE LAND

Agriculture employs about 28 percent of the workforce. This sector is divided into production for local consumption and production for export. In the export sector, bananas are the number one crop, followed by shrimp and cut flowers. Cocoa is also one of the country's main exports. Rice, potatoes, corn, fruits, and other vegetables are produced mainly for domestic consumption.

Bananas are grown on huge estates in the Costa and are mostly exported. Ecuadorians prefer plantains to cook with and do not consume many bananas. Foreign corporations grow cut flowers in the Sierra.

Small farmers grow coffee in the highlands, especially in the south around Loja and in the Oriente. In recent years, the price of coffee has been too low for farmers to make an adequate living, so many are turning to organic and fair-trade coffee production. Fair-trade coffee—produced following certain international criteria, such as a minimum purchase price per pound—fetches much higher prices for the farmers and enables them to develop their communities with the extra money they make.

Throughout the Oriente and Sierra, many peasant families grow fruit and vegetables for their own use and sell the surplus to city dwellers.

Coffee is one of Ecuador's major agricultural products.

LIVESTOCK Ecuadorians tend to raise livestock on small landholdings, primarily for domestic consumption. The people of the Costa and of the Oriente raise mainly beef cattle, grazing their animals on land otherwise unsuitable for agriculture; the residents of the Sierra, called Serranos, raise dairy cattle and graze their animals in the fertile valleys. Many Ecuadorians also raise pigs, sheep, goats, and poultry.

Ceiba trees can grow to 200 feet (61 m) tall.

FISHING Ecuador's ocean border provides a rich resource for coastal residents, and fisheries have become one of the fastest-growing industries in Ecuador. The shrimp industry expanded rapidly during the 1980s and 1990s. As more shrimp were exported from similar industries around the world, the price declined, so shrimp-farming companies responded by intensifying their production. Mangrove forests were ripped up to make way for new ponds, and more shrimp were raised in each pond. From 1998 to 1999, a shrimp disease called white spot swept along the coast, making the harvests unsellable. Some companies are now turning to organic methods to regain their market share.

As well as cultivating shrimp, Ecuadorians also fish the open ocean for export and for domestic consumption.

FORESTRY Ecuador is one of the world's leading exporters of balsa wood. Many Ecuadorians use the forests as a source of fuel and for construction in rural areas. Other products are obtained from Ecuador's trees, such as quinine from cinchona bark, buttons from ivory palm nuts, and mattress stuffing from the silky kapok and fibers from the ceiba (silk-cotton) tree. Forestry has led to extensive deforestation on the coast.

The Trans-Ecuadorian Oil Pipeline is also known as the Sistema de Oleoducto Transecuatoriano (SOTE).

UNDERGROUND RICHES

Ecuador began exploring for oil in the Oriente in the 1920s but did not strike it rich until 1967, when several abundant oil fields were discovered near Nueva Loja (also known as Lago Agrio). Oil companies moved quickly to exploit the reserves, establishing over fifty new oil wells within the next twenty years.

Pipelines transport oil from Nueva Loja across the Andes Mountains to Esmeraldas, where some is refined for domestic consumption and the rest is exported by ship. The first pipeline was built in 1972. In 2003, a second privately owned pipeline was constructed to increase capacity for export. Neither pipeline is running at capacity based on the existing fields, and there is much pressure from industry and those who hold Ecuadorian government debt to expand production into the southern Oriente.

Mining is still a small industry in Ecuador. Gold has traditionally been the most important metal. With mounting pressure to find valuable export products, the government is encouraging foreign mining interests to explore for new deposits in the rich Andes mountain chains. Silver, copper, and gold deposits exist, but not in an amount that would justify large-scale mining operations.

GOODS

Manufacturing accounts for about 13 percent of the country's gross domestic product (GDP), but a significant amount of production takes place in small family businesses. Unlike North America, where most products come from large factories located far away, in Ecuador there are many local craftsmen. For example, every town has a woodworker or furniture maker. Other small local industries include ironmongers who make gates and tools. In large urban centers such as Quito and Guayaquil, there are factories that produce processed foods, clothing, chemicals, cement, and lumber for the domestic market.

OIL: BOOM AND BUST

The Ecuadorian economy is so closely tied to the oil industry that any fluctuations in the price of petroleum can cause ripples felt throughout the nation. In 2009, the price per barrel of crude oil dropped to $30 (compare this to the record high of nearly $130). Ecuador's spending on social programs relies on the money oil brings in, and the government makes up the difference by borrowing from other nations. Thus, when oil prices fall, the country's deficit increases. Recently, Ecuador and China have been forging a closer relationship based on oil and loans. As of 2015, Ecuador has secured billions of dollars from China. These loans have come at a price, though. China now owns 90 percent of Ecuador's oil.

Some industries have suffered due to competition from imported products. The people of Pelileo, for example, were famous for their blue jeans, sewn to mimic all the popular international brands. When Peruvian blue jeans were allowed to enter Ecuador with no tariffs, Pelileo producers could not compete and many closed down. Still, some products are not as easy to transport, so potters producing terra-cotta pots or artisans making wicker baskets have managed to survive in their areas.

SERVICES

Over half of the workforce is employed in the service industry. The main areas of employment are wholesale and retail trade, financial services, transportation, communication, and tourism.

Tourism is growing rapidly in this small country and contributes to the economies of all four regions. Because tourism is widespread and evenly distributed, many small family businesses can benefit from the growth of tourist interest.

TRANSPORTATION Buses and cars are the main modes of transportation, traveling through the countryside on gravel or dirt roads, or along the twisting hairpin turns of Ecuador's highway system. Although many roads become impassable during the rainy season, the major urban centers are

ELECTRONIC CURRENCY

In December 2014, the government of Ecuador adopted a second currency. The Sistema de Dinero Electrónico, or Electronic Money System, is a way for Ecuadorians to complete transactions without ever handing over cash or a credit card. CNBC described the Electronic Money System as: "a government-run version of Venmo—users will be able to make payments with the aid of a cellphone and store value in their accounts. But unlike the popular smartphone application, the Ecuadorean version will be able to run on 'dumb' mobile devices too." The system has led to speculation from economists that the nation's adoption of electronic currency is a way to move toward "de-dollarization," though the entire system is presently tied to the dollar. In 2015, over half a million Ecuadorians adopted the currency, which allows them to pay for everything from taxis to taxes.

connected by all-weather asphalt highways. The Pan-American Highway is the principal highway of Ecuador, following the route of the Inca imperial highway through the Sierra. Four paved highways connect it to the north-south coastal highway.

Railroads were once the primary means of travel within the regions and between the Sierra and the Costa, but the rail system has declined in importance since the 1950s. Air transportation has been developed in recent decades, with 432 airports (2013) throughout the country, though only 104 of these have paved runways. Ecuador has a number of domestic airlines serving local airports, but it no longer has a national airline with international routes.

Ecuador's waterways serve as transportation routes for foreign trade, especially on the coast. Guayaquil is the country's main port. Riverboats and canoes navigate the rivers of the Oriente, serving as the traditional means of transportation to towns and farming areas not reached by roads.

COMMUNICATIONS Cell phones revolutionized communications in Ecuador. Until the past decade, rural areas were virtually unreachable by telephone. The physical barriers of mountains and forests prevented the extension of landlines much beyond populous centers. Today, many Ecuadorians have taken advantage of cellular technology to have reasonably good communication around the country from most vantage points. As of 2014, there's nearly one cell phone per person in Ecuador.

Radio is the traditional means of spreading news and information in rural areas. There are nearly four hundred AM stations throughout the country. In the mountains, their broadcast range is often limited, but they tailor their service to the local areas. Television is popular, and many people pay for satellite service to receive programming from Mexico and Brazil in addition to watching broadcast stations. Most newspapers are big city productions, and the two largest are *El Universo* out of Guayaquil and *El Comercio* published in Quito.

The Pan-American Highway stretches through North and South America.

INTERNET LINKS

www.ft.com/intl/cms/s/0/eb5114d6-d846-11e4-ba53-00144feab7de. html
Mick Conefrey of the *Financial Times* takes a closer look at the cut flower industry of Ecuador in "Roses With Altitude: Why Ecuador's Flower Industry Stands Out."

www.heritage.org/index/country/ecuador
Together the Heritage Foundation and the *Wall Street Journal* maintain a current economic profile of Ecuador.

www.nytimes.com/2015/08/08/opinion/ecuadors-progress.html
The *New York Times*'s website archives a letter to the editor by Francisco Borja Cevallos, the Ambassador of Ecuador. The letter, published in 2015, is the ambassador's account of Ecuador's economic gains.

data.worldbank.org/country/ecuador
Raw economic data and summaries can be found on the World Bank's site.

ENVIRONMENT

The Ecuadorian rain forest is home to spectacular animals, like this blue and yellow macaw.

5

DEPENDING ON WHOM YOU TALK TO, Ecuador is either a leader in environmental conservation or a nation that favors economic opportunity over the environment. However, it is indisputable that Ecuador's government is taking legislative steps to protect the country's plants and animals. Some parts of Ecuador even placed restrictions on bullfighting in a 2011 referendum, citing animal cruelty. Ecuador's amazing landscape is worth protecting—twenty-five thousand plant species and three hundred species of mammals call the country home, not to mention the four thousand species of butterflies! Tourists flock to both mainland Ecuador and the Galápagos Islands for an up-close look at the environmental riches of Ecuador.

There are seventeen countries in the world that are labeled "megadiverse." These countries have an extremely high concentration of biodiversity, and Ecuador is one of them.

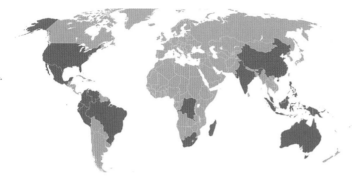

This map shows the world's megadiverse countries.

BIOLOGICAL DIVERSITY

Several factors contribute to making Ecuador a good place for so many kinds of plants and animals. First, low-lying equatorial areas remained warm and habitable through the ice ages, attracting many species that were forced out of their natural habitats by the cold. Second, variations in elevation result in the formation of microclimates. It is colder at higher elevations, and the presence of mountains creates areas of very high and very low rainfall. The combination of varied temperature and rainfall, in turn, forms multiple ecosystems that support different species.

Finally, as a coastal country, Ecuador benefits from the cold Humboldt Current flowing north from Antarctica and the equatorial warm current El Niño. Different species thrive in waters at different temperatures. These factors mean that although Ecuador represents only 0.2 percent of Earth's surface, it has more than its fair share of plants and animals.

ENVIRONMENT VS. ECONOMY

The natural resources of Ecuador are the lifeline of its economy. Yet harvesting these resources comes at the expense of the environment. Some industries have particularly visible effects, such as drilling for oil, growing flowers, and farming shrimp.

OIL The Oriente is the most biodiverse region of the country; it is also the most fragile and threatened. Tropical rain forests do not easily recover when destroyed. Unfortunately, this is also where Ecuadorian oil lies deep beneath the surface, and it is the least populated habitable region of the country. These two facts threaten the region's environmental integrity.

When oil was discovered in the northeast, near Lago Agrio, by Texaco (now Chevron Texaco), massive drilling in the area began. Texaco left in 1992, but much of the northeast had by then been opened to oil exploration and drilling. Pumping oil is a messy business, and there are always great risks of environmental contamination from spills.

After over fifty years of oil development, the Oriente is devastated and the indigenous Cofán people nearly extinct. Their population fell from around fifteen thousand in the late 1960s and early 1970s to two thousand today (although this number is the total Cofán population in Ecuador and Colombia). Rates of childhood leukemia and spontaneous miscarriages are above regional averages here, and many people have had to move to avoid polluted waters and soil. The damage extends to the Pacific. In 2003, ten thousand barrels of oil spilled into Quito's main water reservoir, Laguna Papallacta, when a pipeline ruptured.

In addition, the construction of roads was needed in order to reach the best drilling sites. New roads also gave loggers and settlers access to pristine forest. The government has encouraged people from the highlands and the

Protesters march against Chevron Texaco in 2014.

Oil spills in the rain forest are devastating to people and wildlife.

coast to move to the Oriente to farm. Farming thin tropical soils is difficult, so settlers are forced to clear new land every few years to maintain crop and livestock yields. They move farther into nature preserves, pristine wilderness, and indigenous territories, destroying the ecosystem along the way.

The construction of a second oil pipeline, the OCP, resulted in environmental damage all along its route, crossing eleven protected areas.

CUT FLOWERS Near Cayambe, north of Quito, a unique industry sprang up in the early 2000s to help Ecuador meet its loan obligations to foreign debtors—cut flowers. Many of the long-stemmed roses in North American florist shops come from the highland areas of Ecuador and Colombia. Growing greenhouse flowers requires careful control of light, temperature, pests, and water. Flower growers typically use high concentrations of pesticides and often compete with local farmers for limited supplies of irrigation water.

Amphibians in Ecuador run the gamut from innocuous to poisonous. Over four hundred species of frogs make their home in Ecuador—and counting. In 2009, a new species of frog was discovered in the Andes. The "transformer frog" (scientific name Pristimantis mutabilis*) has a unique reaction when facing predators. The frog's skin changes to become spiny.*

Aside from the "transformer frog," there's been more exciting amphibian news out of Ecuador in recent years. The Azuay stubfoot toad (right) was declared extinct in 2002 but rediscovered in 2015. This species of toad had become infected by a kind of fungus that decimated other species of amphibian.

Yet not all the news related to amphibians is good news. Many species are now on endangered species lists, and conservationists are fighting to save them. Groups like the Amphibian Specialist Group, Amphibian Survival Alliance, and the Rainforest Trust have joined together to designate amphibians' natural habitats as protected land.

Local farmers can no longer grow their traditional crops because they cannot irrigate their fields. In addition, the pesticides used on the flowers make their way into the water system and into workers' bodies, causing health problems and damaging local flora and fauna.

There are other concerns, especially regarding the number of child laborers working in this industry. Many children work during the school year—as many as 13 percent, most of them in agriculture. There has been increased pressure by nations worldwide to get Ecuador to stop child labor. In 2005, Ecuador launched reforms to limit the number of children working; however, as of 2015, many child workers still exist.

SHRIMP FARMING The coast has not escaped the problems of resource extraction and environmental damage. Since the 1980s, coastal mangrove forests near Guayaquil and Esmeraldas have been ripped up to make way for shrimp ponds. Species of shellfish that live in the mangroves are destroyed, as are the livelihoods of local people who harvest them to make a living. Shrimp are farmed intensively in large pools that must be fed a combination of fresh and salt water. The shrimp are treated with huge doses of antibiotics to prevent the spread of disease. When the water from the pools is emptied at harvest time, drug-laced water feeds into coastal estuaries, harming native species.

GRASSROOTS EFFORTS

Some Ecuadorians, though not the majority, are increasingly aware of the value of healthy and pristine environments. At the local level, they have begun to organize to protect their natural patrimony, both because it is valuable in itself and because tourists are willing to pay to experience it.

Indigenous groups in the Oriente have joined together in a group called CONFENIAE, which lobbies the government to set high environmental standards for companies wishing to do business in Ecuador's oil patch. Some member groups have successfully prevented oil company workers from entering their land, while others permit oil development but insist that companies consult with them and pay them for access to their lands. The Cofán went a step further and sued Chevron Texaco for its careless destruction of their lands and health. The case was heard in Ecuador and the people won. In 2011, Chevron Texaco was ordered to pay $9.5 billion in cleanup costs, although this judgment is unenforceable because American courts have thrown out the ruling.

Across the country, some locals are creating innovative strategies for opposing destruction of the environment and pursuing sustainable strategies for living, though many groups have faced opposition from the Correa administration. Correa's government has shut down several environmental groups during his time in office. Correa says that these groups—such as the Pachamama Foundation and Acción Ecológica—are either a threat to public

OASES OF BEAUTY

Ecuador has eleven national parks and more than twenty nature preserves. These span from the Costa in the west to the Amazon basin in the east. The Galápagos Islands are probably the most famous national park, but there is plenty more to see on the mainland. In the Cuyabeno Nature Reserve, near the border with Colombia and Peru, pink freshwater dolphins play in the rivers. They give birth to live young and reach 8.25 to 9.75 feet (2.5 to 3 m) in length at maturity. They spend a lot of time foraging for food alone. They can turn their heads 180 degrees, which helps them find fish among tree roots in flooded rivers. They have no predators but are threatened by pollution and habitat destruction.

In the Cayambe-Coca Ecological Reserve, northeast of Quito, some of Ecuador's last condors grace the skies. They are the largest flying birds in the world and can fly as high as 16,000 feet (4,877 m). They eat dead animals, but many farmers believe they threaten livestock. Condors have been hunted nearly to extinction—fewer than one hundred remain in Ecuador.

On the coast, Machalilla National Park hosts a fantastic array of birds. The park includes Isla de la Plata (Silver Island), often called the "Poor Man's Galápagos" because it has many of the seabirds found on the Galápagos but is much cheaper to visit. One seabird found here is the blue-footed booby. It has blue feet, and the name "booby" comes from the Spanish word bobo *(boh-boh), which means "stupid." It earned this unfortunate name because it tends to be clumsy on land and performs entertaining mating rituals involving lifting one foot and then the other. However, watching a booby dive into the ocean or catch flying fish in midair proves that these birds are anything but stupid or clumsy.*

order or lack the proper legal statuses as nongovernmental organizations (NGOs). Still, some effective environmental NGOs remain in operation, such as the Fundación Natura.

ECOTOURISM AND GLOBAL ACTIVISM

Environmental conflicts result from Ecuador's dependence on natural resources as a source of national wealth. As lenders such as the International Monetary Fund have increased pressure on the government to pay back its loans, destructive extractive industry has been encouraged if it produces a

high-value product for sale on international markets. The health of Ecuador's environment is dependent on the demands of outside financial institutions, on consumers who are willing to pay for these damaging products, and on the foreign companies who make money from Ecuador's natural resources.

While foreign companies have contributed to environmental destruction, foreign tourists have turned out to be great allies of local environmentalists. Americans, Canadians, Italians, and Germans have all worked with Ecuadorian nongovernmental organizations to inform the world about the damage done by the OCP pipeline and by oil extraction in general. After seeing the beauty and the destruction firsthand, tourists have returned home to try to make a difference. They have mounted information and boycott campaigns against the companies involved, and at least some of these companies have decided to pull out rather than risk further embarrassment. Shareholders in companies such as Chevron Texaco are demanding that the company take responsibility for its actions.

Environmental groups are working to create and enforce standards for the cut-flower industry so that greenhouses practicing safe and reduced pesticide use while protecting their workers can sell their flowers in an environmentally friendly way. Other groups lobby to have foreign debt forgiven or reduced so that countries like Ecuador do not have to mortgage nature to pay their bills. Defending Ecuador's megadiversity has become a global affair.

Another alternative to destructive industry and agriculture is ecotourism, which provides a living for people and encourages environmental preservation. Increasingly, the business of preserving Ecuador's unique environments has become a global concern, attracting attention from people all over the world who have had the pleasure of experiencing megadiversity up close. The combination of local and international initiatives is a good starting point for an environmentally friendly economy and future.

INTERNET LINKS

www.geo.cornell.edu/geology/GalapagosWWW/Darwin.html
Cornell University provides a "Brief History of the Galapagos," which includes information about Charles Darwin's famous expedition.

www.nature.org/ourinitiatives/regions/southamerica/ecuador
Find videos, the latest news, and articles about conservation efforts in Ecuador on the Nature Conservancy's site.

www.worldwildlife.org/places/the-galapagos
The World Wildlife Fund provides an overview of the Galápagos Islands, photos, videos, and an explanation of the environmental threats the Galápagos face.

ECUADORIANS

The vibrancy of Ecuador stems from its diverse people.

6

A S WITH MANY COUNTRIES, IT'S difficult to point to one unifying Ecuadorian identity. Ecuador's population inhabits wildly different landscapes and Ecuadorians have varied demographic backgrounds. The blend of languages, customs, and arts found in Ecuador is unparalleled. While these differences have led to a hierarchical society, marginalized groups are finding ways to advocate for themselves and level the playing field.

Immigration and emigration also contribute to the unique makeup of Ecuador's population. Refugees from Colombia constitute around 98 percent of Ecuador's immigrant population, and Ecuadorians who left the country in the 1990s for better economic opportunities are now returning to their homeland as the world economy struggles.

SOCIAL STRATIFICATION

Broadly speaking, the small economic, political, and intellectual elite considers themselves to be white and descended directly from the original Spanish colonial settlers. However, Lebanese Ecuadorians have risen up through the social ranks to become successful economically and

Ecuador's population includes indigenous peoples, Afro-Ecuadorians (descended from African slaves), white Ecuadorians (descended from the first Spanish settlers), and the descendants of more recent immigrant groups. Mestizos are descended from European and indigenous unions.

politically. Two presidents in the 1990s, Jamil Mahuad and Abdalá Bucaram, were Lebanese Ecuadorians.

The slightly larger middle class includes people of a number of different ethnic identities. There are whites who are not wealthy in money or land, but who work as high-level civil servants and professionals or form part of the intellectual elite of writers, artists, and university professors. Many mestizos—or half Spanish half indigenous people—are also middle class and make up the bulk of the civil service ranks, work as professionals, or own small businesses.

Some Native communities have capitalized on the international demand for their colorful woven goods, and those who have become exporters or retailers are firmly middle class in terms of education, income, and economic security. Afro-Ecuadorians generally live in the northwestern coastal plain; some are middle class, running small businesses or working as professionals.

The largest social stratum is the poor. Estimates of the number of people living in poverty range from 25 to 35 percent of the population. This large section of the population is mostly indigenous, mestizo, and Afro-Ecuadorian. For this reason, it is often assumed that the majority of indigenous people are poor, but while it is true that many poor people are indigenous, many are also mestizo and some are of African descent.

Poverty is experienced differently in the city and in the countryside. In the city, the poor do manual work such as construction or domestic service, when they are lucky to find regular employment. These are the people living in inadequate housing on the fringes of Quito, Guayaquil, and other large urban centers. Many come to the city to escape even harsher conditions in the countryside, where farmland is scarce and paid work is seasonal and vastly underpaid.

Because there has never been really effective land reform in Ecuador, the most productive land is still owned by the elite. This leaves many rural people, Afro-Ecuadorian, mestizo, and indigenous, with little or no land to farm. Without land and without opportunities for work, the rural poor move to the cities to try their luck there.

PREJUDICE

During colonial and early republican times, ethnicity was the single most important determinant of life opportunities. Being born white, mestizo, black, or indigenous determined what sort of life you could expect to lead. White Ecuadorians had little respect for indigenous cultures and used many insulting terms to refer to non-white Ecuadorians. This pattern of prejudice was widespread well into the twentieth century, and remnants of it are still seen today.

However, in the last decades, indigenous peoples have begun to organize and educate themselves to challenge these prejudices. At the same time, Ecuadorians in general have begun to appreciate their twin heritages of European and Native cultures. Whereas in the past, indigenous people often struggled to become mestizo and mestizos worked hard to be accepted as whites, today there is less pressure to disguise one's ethnicity and much more pride among young indigenous peoples across the country.

It may seem odd that people could change their ethnic identity, but it was possible because many of the characteristics that distinguish one group from the other are not physical as much as social. For example, whites are not always fair skinned, but they are people who trace their descent to Spanish settlers through their Spanish last names. They also speak Spanish as a first language and are highly educated. Mestizos also wear Western clothing but are generally not as wealthy and not as well educated as whites. Some mestizo families still have one indigenous last name, though most speak Spanish as their home language. Without clothing or other social indicators like language or job, it can be very difficult to tell if a person is mestizo or indigenous. For that reason, indigenous people who wanted to change their social identity could simply perfect their Spanish, usually their second language, change the way they dressed, and get a better education or job in order to fit in. Previously, they would also have dropped their indigenous names.

Today indigenous city dwellers often adopt Western clothing, and most young indigenous Ecuadorians speak fluent Spanish, but they do not feel the same pressure to hide their cultural heritage because there is less prejudice against them. In fact, some indigenous communities are reasserting their cultural traditions and distinctiveness with pride. In the southern Sierra, mestizos sometimes change their affiliation to join the indigenous communities, such as the Saraguro, as a means of improving their economic status.

INDIGENOUS PEOPLES

There are indigenous groups in all three mainland regions of Ecuador. The smallest group—around 9 percent of the total indigenous population—lives in the Costa and consists of the Colorado, the Cayapa, and the Coaiquer. The forest-dwelling Colorado make a living primarily by fishing, hunting, and farming. The Cayapa and the Colorado speak dialects of the Chibcha language, while the Coaiquer speak a separate language altogether. Coastal indigenous communities have dwindled due to migration and assimilation with mestizo culture.

Indigenous women in Saraguro celebrate Easter.

A few million indigenous people live in the Sierra region. Precise numbers are impossible because the Ecuadorian government does not collect census information by ethnicity. Nonetheless, this is where the bulk of Native Ecuadorians live.

All Sierran indigenous peoples speak Quechua. The Incas moved groups of people from Bolivia and elsewhere in the Inca Empire to the Ecuadorian Sierra as a means of introducing Quechua, along with the Inca religion and ways of life. Within this group are a number of separate ethnic and cultural subgroups. For example, the Salasaca people were moved to the central Sierra, and the Saraguro people were moved to the southern Sierra.

These subgroups mark their differences in their dress. Typically, the color of a man's poncho, the kind of hats worn by men and women, the style of women's skirts, the type of jewelry, and hairstyles mark distinctions between these subgroups. It is said that the Saraguro men wear their black ponchos in continuous mourning for the last Sapa Inca, who was killed by the Spanish conquerors.

Sierran indigenous peoples are expert farmers. With generations of experience, they know the precise climatic conditions necessary to grow a number of different crops in the diverse mountain terrain. Potatoes grow high up the mountainsides, vegetables on the lower slopes, and corn thrives in the warmer mountain valleys.

Despite centuries of domination by colonial and republican elite, Sierrans have retained many of their customs. Working together with Oriente indigenous peoples, Sierrans have established powerful political organizations to force the elite-dominated government to take their concerns seriously.

Oriente indigenous peoples are divided into several language groups, including Shuara speakers and Kichwa speakers. Kichwa is a dialect of highland Quechua that was probably diffused to the lowlands after the Spanish conquest.

Oriente indigenous cultures include the Shuar, Ashuar, Waorani, Cofán, Siona-Secoya, and Zaparoan. The Tetete people were virtually exterminated by contamination of their lands caused by oil operations in the 1970s.

Lowland peoples traditionally survived by slash-and-burn tropical agriculture, hunting, fishing, and gathering. Today, some groups still practice

Otavaleños are the Sierran indigenous inhabitants of a town north of Quito called Otavalo. They may be Ecuador's most famous indigenous group because they have defied prejudice and inequality to create economically and socially sustainable lifestyles.

Historically, the people of Otavalo raised sheep for wool and were forced by colonial authorities to process the wool into textiles under a form of semi-slavery. This expertise in dying and weaving wool has served Otavaleños well.

Since Ecuador began to attract international tourists in greater numbers in the 1980s, foreigners have been captivated by the colorful weavings of Otavalo. At first, clever foreigners started buying these weavings to sell in their home countries, but Otavaleños quickly realized that they could make more money if they marketed their own goods abroad. Some families were able to amass small fortunes by getting together enough money to pay for one of their members to travel abroad to sell handicrafts from the area. Now, successful Otavaleños travel abroad as often as the richest Ecuadorians, and some have begun to buy up rural land and urban property in surrounding cities. They control their town council and have worked hard to educate their young people, not so they can move to Quito but so they can form a local professional class.

Otavaleño parents take pains to make sure their children are fully bilingual in Quechua and Spanish, but they retain their distinctive dress as a sign of pride in their identity. Men typically wear reversible dark blue and tan or gray ponchos with short-cropped white trousers, white shirts, felt hats, and rope-soled sandals. Women wear dark blue wrap skirts, embroidered white blouses, woolen shawls, and rope sandals. The women always carry an extra piece of blue wool material that can serve as another shawl if it is cold or as head protection if it is hot or raining. Women also wear gold glass necklaces and bracelets of red beads.

their traditional subsistence strategies, but only if they live far enough from encroachment by highland and coastal peasants seeking land, or from extractive oil and mining industries.

Oriente indigenous peoples have formed an integral part of the modern indigenous political movement in Ecuador. In the last three decades, they have entered public life, sometimes dramatically, by organizing marches to Quito to demonstrate for their rights.

AFRO-ECUADORIANS

Approximately 4 percent of Ecuadorians are descendants of African slaves who were brought to Ecuador in colonial times to work on coastal sugar plantations. Some arrived by escaping from shipwrecked slave ships and survived by integrating with coastal indigenous peoples. Their descendants live primarily in the northern coastal region around Esmeraldas, but there is also a highland community in the Sierran town of Chota.

While most people of African descent in South America have long since lost their original West African languages and cultures, this heritage is still observable in their musical, spoken, and religious traditions. Among the

These Afro-Ecuadorian athletes are training in Valle del Chota.

African traditions that Chota Valley inhabitants have retained are African-style thatch roofing for their houses and the colorful headscarves worn by Chota women.

Today, Afro-Ecuadorians are moving more and more into mainstream life in Guayaquil and Quito, and they are inspiring a newfound appreciation for their distinctive traditions and histories.

WHITE ECUADORIANS

Blancos (blan-kohs), or whites, are a small part of the population. Their culture is the dominant one in the country, but it has changed dramatically in the last forty to fifty years. Whites all speak Spanish as their first language, but English is increasingly seen as an important language to know to get ahead. Imported clothing from Europe and the United States, international travel, and foreign education are part of elite white Ecuadorian culture. Whites continue to dominate the highest levels of government and business in the country.

Private schools often teach English to their pupils.

PATRIOTISM

It might be surprising that a nation with so many unique cultures and varied lifestyles is known as a deeply patriotic country, but in Ecuador, citizens are proud of their shared heritage. Ecuadorians are known for their patriotism. Statues honoring the founders of the country can be found in many public squares, and bank holidays celebrate the nation's route to independence.

COMING TOGETHER

Ecuador is a society divided along many lines: linguistic, cultural, economic, and regional. Historical circumstances have put some groups on top and others at the bottom of the social scale. Recently, indigenous peoples have begun to reassert their pride and establish a place for themselves in public life. Many Ecuadorians welcome this change and are working toward creating a more inclusive national culture.

INTERNET LINKS

www.aljazeera.com/indepth/opinion/2012/08/201285142554706344. html
In this article about hip-hop music performed in a mix of Spanish and the Kichwa language, *Al Jazeera* debunks the idea that indigenous people lead antiquated lives.

www.nmai.si.edu/searchcollections/results.aspx?regid=428
This website includes a searchable collection of Native American artifacts. Shuar ornaments are just one part of the museum's digitized holdings.

www.roughguides.com/destinations/south-america/ecuador/ culture-etiquette
Rough Guides' "Ecuador: Culture and Etiquette" offers observations about the cultural norms of the nation.

LIFESTYLE

Quito is made up of modern and traditional buildings, some brightly colored.

7

ECUADORIAN LIFE REVOLVES AROUND tight-knit, multi-generational families. Families are instrumental in marking rites of passage common to most cultural groups in Ecuador. Milestone birthdays, birth, and marriage entail distinct customs. These events are celebrated in churches or with ritualized ceremonies in indigenous communities. Food plays a prominent role in special occasions. Day-to-day life in Ecuador also involves sharing meals together as a family.

Home is where the family congregates after work, school, and on weekends or during holidays. Friendship is also important, especially *compadrazgo* (kom-pah-DRAHZ-goh), or godparent relationships.

The daily routines of Ecuadorians in the city sharply contrast with those living in the country, yet all Ecuadorians have great national pride no matter the region in which they live.

CITY LIFE

Houses in the cities are generally built close to one another. Middle- and upper-class people often barricade themselves behind secure, solid metal or wrought-iron gates and tall stone walls topped with shards of glass and other sharp objects. Houses in the Costa are usually made of wood and often stand on stilts in order to withstand heavy flooding. Because of the pervasive use of wood as a building material

Traditional homes in Cuenca date back to colonial times.

in Guayaquil, many historical buildings, especially churches, have been lost to fire over the centuries.

Although middle- and upper-class Ecuadorians value their relationships with family and friends, they generally do not socialize with their neighbors. Their houses are usually two or three stories high, surrounded by tall fences that enclose a back courtyard or lawn. Older colonial-style houses display a rectangular form of architecture, arranged around an open-air courtyard in the center of the structure, with second-floor verandas or balconies overlooking the central area.

The majority of these houses include servant's quarters adjacent to the laundry and kitchen areas. From this location, the servant can reach work areas without walking through the main rooms of the house. The bottom floor of the house, aside from the kitchen and the servant's quarters, generally is used only for entertaining company. The family usually eats together in the kitchen and leaves the dining room for formal occasions. Likewise, the *sala*, or main room of the house, is unoccupied most of the time. The family spends much of its leisure time at home in the bedrooms, especially the main bedroom, where the television is located. The *señora*, or lady of the house, even entertains friends in her bedroom.

In contrast, the urban poor often move into dilapidated and abandoned houses. They generally lack sewage facilities, electricity, and running water. They might also build makeshift shacks from scrap materials, adobe, reed, or cane.

COUNTRY LIFE

Rural houses are generally made from materials such as bamboo, adobe, packed earth, wattle and daub, or wood. In the Sierra, people build their houses as solidly as possible to withstand the cold; adobe brick houses

This bungalow is a good example of a *campesino* house.

Traditional Waorani houses take advantage of natural materials.

topped with thatch roofs are a common sight. In recent years, many *campesinos* (agricultural workers) have begun to roof their houses with metal sheeting, but they are finding that these materials are not as well suited to their environment as the traditional thatch roofing. In the Costa, campesinos and wage laborers construct their houses of wood or bamboo and mount them on stilts to withstand flooding. Rural houses throughout Ecuador are often located in remote areas, such as the high páramo, the base of a volcano, the thick, swampy lowlands, or the jungle rain forest.

Country houses for the wealthy display graceful verandas, balconies, and frescos. The buildings often surround a central courtyard, which may include a small, decorative fish pond or beautiful flower banks. Extensive gardens generally surround the exterior of the structure, often featuring strutting peacocks or parrots. A large brick wall and heavy gate protect the estate from passersby. Many of the old *haciendas* (ah-see-EHN-dahs) in the Sierra have been sold and are now used as resorts. In addition to the enormous size of the main building and its surrounding yard, several other buildings usually occupy the estate, such as stables and barns.

The Waorani in the Oriente build their well-ventilated houses from palm fronds and waterproof broad leaves, which they lash to frames made from stripped saplings. The result is an elongated, dome-shaped structure that can house more than ten people in its single room. Since Waorani communities are usually very small, only a few houses are needed.

The Shuar construct their large, oval-shaped wooden houses as defensive strongholds against attacks by their enemies. They build the walls, without windows, from wooden posts that are stuck vertically into the ground about

1 inch (2.54 centimeters) apart, thus permitting light and air to enter the large room inside. They thatch the roof with closely woven palm leaves. The houses are constructed on a rise, which allows the residents to observe the surrounding area for intruders, as well as offering better drainage. Each family lives in isolation from its neighbors and extended family. The houses range from about 25 to 36 feet (7 to 11 m) in width and from 40 to 60 feet (12 to 18 m) in length.

POPULATION SHIFTS

Once a primarily rural country with its major population base in the Sierra, Ecuador has experienced a radical population shift in the last fifty to sixty years. First, large numbers of landless and land-poor campesinos from the Sierra began flocking to the Costa from 1950 to 1974, looking for work in export agriculture. Also beginning in 1950, large numbers of Serranos migrated to the Oriente. Between 1950 and 1982, the population of the Oriente increased fivefold.

At the same time, thousands more migrated to the cities. Guayaquil attracted campesinos looking for work in export agriculture during the banana boom. Quito later drew migrants looking for work during the oil boom. Land reform efforts initiated the process to some degree; as the supply of wage laborers increased, it became more difficult to find agricultural work in the Sierra. The rapid increase in urban populations resulted in an explosion of shantytowns around major cities.

TRADITIONAL ROLES

The dominant Ecuadorian culture derives from traditions brought from Spain. Although women enjoyed many rights in the sixteenth and seventeenth centuries, in the eighteenth century the man became the head of the family and assumed absolute authority over his wife and children. This is still the dominant gender-role model in Ecuador today. Women are ideally feminine and oriented to their roles as a loving mother and a dutiful wife. However, in contemporary Ecuador, these gender roles and expectations are changing.

Given the economic instability and upheaval in recent decades, many more Ecuadorian women of the middle class now work full- or part-time jobs to supplement the family income. They dominate the fields of teaching, nursing, and office work but are increasingly found in other spheres, too. Poor women have always had to work in the fields in rural areas or in menial jobs in the cities. Many will do domestic work for richer families, while others are street vendors. Many rich women still adhere to the gender expectation that they will remain at home to raise their children and care for their families, but they are a very small percentage of the population.

With the expectation that they will work some or most of their lives, many more young Ecuadorian women now pursue post-secondary education in the universities or vocational schools. They are choosing careers in non-traditional professions such as law and medicine.

In contemporary Ecuadorian families, women often contribute to the household income and likewise to household decisions. Working mothers strive to maintain the maternal ideal while balancing work obligations outside the home. However, both genders value their parental roles and both mothers and fathers are generally affectionate with their children.

Among Sierran indigenous groups, men and women are seen to be halves of a whole with complementary roles. Neither is dominant since both are necessary for the functioning of the family. Publicly, indigenous women may defer to their husbands but they are strong partners in their marriages and are valued for their contribution to home life. Both men and women are bound by strict rules of fidelity and respect.

MARRIAGE

The marriage ceremony is taken very seriously in Ecuador. Many of the country's population celebrate with a ceremony. Most devout Ecuadorians will have a traditional church wedding—usually a Catholic service—while indigenous or non-religious people may have civil ceremonies, which are recognized by the state. Many of these ceremonies resemble weddings in the United States, complete with a bride in a white dress, walking down an aisle, and an after party. Some indigenous people celebrate in their own wedding

GENDER INEQUALITY

Ecuadorian women do not yet enjoy equal rights with men despite the fact that in 1929 Ecuador was the first country in South America to give women the right to vote. Recent legislation has improved their legal rights, but laws cannot guarantee compliance. For example, the 1998 constitution emphasized the equality of the sexes, but women are still paid less than men for equal work and are not treated the same as men in public life.

Poor women and rural women face the biggest challenges. In poor rural areas, families need the labor of their children to survive. If there is enough money left over to afford education for only one or two children, boys are favored because it is believed they have a better chance to get well-paid work. This means that while Ecuador's overall literacy rate seems high at 94.5 percent, many poor women cannot read beyond a very basic level.

The economic crises of the 1990s made women's lives even more difficult. As families fell deeper into poverty and stress, violence and abandonment were common consequences. Additionally, alcohol abuse is very often the cause of family violence. A law against domestic violence was passed in 1995, and then strengthened in 2007, but not all women are aware of their rights under this law and many lack access to legal resources to have the law enforced. A second problem has emerged in recent years as poorer Ecuadorians have migrated to Spain, Italy, and other parts of Europe and to the United States seeking work. All too commonly, male migrants start off by sending money home to their wives and children but then find a new partner in their adopted country and simply stop all communication and support. The laws defending a woman's right to spousal support are weakly enforced within the country and there is no way to make them work over such long distances.

Fortunately, many men and women are actively working to change these circumstances. There are groups offering legal aid and rights education in poor areas. In 2000, a new law mandated that at least 30 percent of all political candidates running for office had to be women. The law was incorporated into the latest constitution, giving women greater direct access to the halls of government.

ceremonies and in traditional ceremonial dress. During one's lifetime, it is likely that many people will experience two or more marriages, as divorce is becoming increasingly common.

In Ecuador, many young people live with their parents before getting married. Most people marry between twenty and thirty years old, although they begin dating as early as age fifteen. In Esmeraldas, courtship is generally brief, and premarital cohabitation is common. Many Ecuadorian men often have several marriages in their lifetime. Esmeraldeños have begun to unite in religious ceremonies only within the last few decades; the men have generally been unwilling to have a religious ceremony because of the commitment it implies.

Although Waorani men traditionally obtained spouses through spearing raids, it is more common today to seek spouses through peaceful interaction with other Waorani groups, who may live 60 miles (96 km) away or more through dense jungle. Waorani also increasingly intermarry with Kichwa-speaking people of the lowland Oriente.

FAMILY STRUCTURE

Indigenous and nonindigenous Ecuadorians alike place great value on the family, which consists of the immediate family unit as well as extended family and others, such as godparents. A single household usually consists of the mother, father, and their unmarried children, as well as one or more members of the extended family. Newly married couples often live with one of the sets of parents for a short period, and the youngest son and his wife often continue to live at home to take care of his parents in their later years.

The wider net of kinship serves as a source of support and assistance. Upper-class families increase their power and prestige through the cultivation of far-reaching kinship ties. Lower-class families try to cultivate and strengthen those kinship ties that will be most beneficial and least costly to them. At all levels, ties are maintained through mutual gift giving, exchanging of favors, and participation at family and community fiestas.

Members of all ethnic groups seek kinship ties outside the network of their extended families, primarily through the godparent system. Godparents, or *compadres* (kohm-PAHD-rays), are highly honored. Although an individual might argue or express disagreement with another family member, it would be unthinkable to treat a compadre in such a way.

CELEBRATING NEW LIFE

The birth of a child is greeted with joyous celebration and ritual ceremony. In a Catholic family, the child is usually baptized as a baby, sometimes within days of the birth. The baptism is celebrated with feasting, drinking, and dancing among the rest of the family. At this time, the baby acquires a first set of compadres, who pledge to bear the responsibility of providing the child with a Christian education and upbringing. Also through this ritual, the parents and the compadres establish a lifelong relationship that persists even if the child dies.

The child also receives a personal patron saint, whose fiesta day the child will celebrate throughout life, often to a greater degree than the child's own birthday.

Among the Shuar, a baby is given a mild hallucinogenic drug within a few days of the birth. This is meant to help the baby see a vision that might give him or her supernatural powers and help in survival.

RITES OF PASSAGE

The first religious ceremony in which Catholic whites and indigenous children consciously participate is that of First Communion. Children around the age of seven make their first confession to cleanse them in preparation for receiving their First Communion. They dress in white, symbolizing purity.

As in much of South America, most girls participate in a ceremony and fiesta known as the *quinceañera* (keen-see-NYA-rah) upon reaching their fifteenth birthday. This is considered their initiation into womanhood. The celebration takes place through the church and is often quite elaborate. The girl wears a formal dress and receives Communion from the priest or minister. Her father stands at her side, as he would at her wedding. The accompanying feasting and drinking costs a great deal of money, even with the simplest arrangements. Parents often have to borrow money and become heavily indebted, especially if they have more than one daughter for whom to celebrate.

SHUAR FAMILY STRUCTURE

The Shuar family structure is unique in Ecuador, primarily because it is polygamous, and secondly because it does not always preserve kinship ties among the extended family. Each household is very closely knit in social and economic terms. The family usually lives in relative isolation from other families in the tribe, with at least 0.5 miles (0.8 km) between dwellings.

The typical household consists of approximately ten people, including one husband, at least two wives, and about seven children. Other relatives, such as a widowed mother or unmarried brother, may also live in the house. Usually when one of the daughters marries, her husband also moves into the house until their first child is born, unless he is already married and must return home with his second wife.

The man is the head of the household and appears as a rather authoritarian figure within the family. He is responsible for providing for and protecting the family by hunting and fishing, clearing the forest for gardens, and bringing in firewood. The role of the woman, or women, is to carry out agricultural tasks, cook the meals, make manioc beer and pottery, and take care of the children and livestock.

Young Shuar girls also undergo a ceremony of initiation, although at a much younger age. The girl is administered the same mild hallucinogenic plant she received when she was born, together with a little tobacco water. The purpose is for the girl to acquire spiritual power so that when she is older she will be able to work hard and be successful producing children and raising crops, chickens, and pigs. Several girls, usually about six, participate together in the ceremony, which is marked by four days of feasting and dancing at the house of the host father. For a week beforehand, the girls observe strict dietary practices, including the avoidance of any meat from mammals or birds. On the first day, the girls dance until midafternoon. Then they consume the drug and lie down at nightfall to experience visions of bountiful crops, chickens, and pigs, while the adults dance and drink until dawn. This process is repeated for the next three nights.

Shuar boys are taken to the highest waterfall at about the age of six in order to help them see visions and begin seeking spiritual power. The spray of the waterfall is believed to contain certain souls or spirits.

THE SCHOOL YEARS

Education in Ecuador is compulsory for children between six and fourteen years of age, although attendance is not enforced. Approximately 18 percent of the schools are run by the Catholic Church, by foreign organizations, and by Protestant missionaries.

Children can start preschool when they are four years old. Most children, however, begin attending school at age six for their primary education. After this, they may advance to secondary school, which consists of two cycles of three years each. The first three years expand on the primary schooling through a general education program. For the second three-year cycle, students can choose to take the university path by obtaining an education in the humanities or to prepare for technical school or teacher training.

After graduating from secondary school, those with sufficient means attend a university. Universities are either private or public. Public institutions

Girls attending a friend's *quinceañera.*

The institution of compadrazgo among indigenous and non-Native Christians is considered to be supremely important. Godparents are chosen not only at birth, but also at confirmation and marriage. At each occasion, the compadres agree to assume ritual and financial obligations to the child or to the newly married couple, as well as to their parents. The relationship is considered sacred.

Many indigenous and mestizo campesinos ask wealthy and influential whites to serve as godparents to their children. Relationships in this system of patronage are complex and mutually beneficial, involving loyalty and support. It is not unusual for wealthy godparents to have several godchildren, which serves to increase their own prestige. Or parents may choose compadres of an equal status, in which case the level of mutual obligations and gift giving between the parents and godparents balances out.

are more affordable, but private schools are considered more prestigious. Additionally, there are more than three hundred private and vocational institutes for post-secondary training.

Although educational opportunities have expanded considerably, there is still a gap in the opportunities available to rural children. Many children living in the countryside and some living in cities are unable to attend school because their families need them to supplement the family income or assist in agricultural work. In the countryside, this may mean sowing seeds, spinning wool, or tending livestock. In the urban areas, street children often shine shoes or sell candy and crafts.

MOURNING

Funerals are generally solemn affairs in Ecuador, especially if a child has died. When a child dies, he is known as an *angelito* (ahn-hay-LEE-toh) and is believed to ascend directly to heaven. Traditional funeral foods in the Sierra include *cuy* (kwee), or guinea pig, which is roasted whole and served with a sauce. However, these are no longer commonly consumed by rural people and are rarely eaten in the cities and towns.

In the communities of Esmeraldas, funerals for adults are solemn and accompanied by specific songs. The local kin hold a wake, in which they lay the body, either at home or in church, on a table covered with a white cloth. They place flowers, leaves, and white crepe-paper wreaths on the chest of the deceased. Singers perform special songs, and the entire tone of the gathering is mournful. Close female relatives may weep openly. The next day, the priest at the cemetery leads a short burial ceremony.

Nine days of mourning follow the burial, during which the windows and doors of the house are left open—more likely in the countryside than in the cities and towns—so the ghost can depart and also so it can return. On the ninth day, the entire group of relatives from far and wide gathers together to bid farewell to the deceased. The farewell ceremony is accompanied by more mournful singing, which continues until it is believed that ties with the deceased have been severed.

INTERNET LINKS

news.bbc.co.uk/2/shared/spl/hi/picture_gallery/05/americas_school _for_ecuador_indigenous_women/html/1.stm
"In Pictures: School for Ecuador's Indigenous Women" is a photo essay that includes interviews with indigenous women pursuing school in adulthood.

www.quinceanera.com/traditions/different-countries-cultures-different-quince-traditions
Quinceanera.com compares traditional ways of celebrating quinceañeras around the world, including the customs of Ecuador.

www.ruralpovertyportal.org/country/home/tags/ecuador
The International Fund for Agricultural Development's report looks at the realities of poverty in rural Ecuador.

RELIGION

The Basilica of the National Vow is a great example of the country's beautiful places of worship.

8

RELIGION PLAYS A CENTRAL ROLE IN life in Ecuador. Almost 75 percent of Ecuadorians identify as Roman Catholic, a religion brought by the Spanish in the sixteenth century. However, the current percentage of Roman Catholics in Ecuador has actually declined. In the 1990s and 2000s, an overwhelming majority of the population—90 percent—was Catholic.

Catholicism has become so deeply ingrained in Ecuadorian society that even people unaffiliated with the Catholic Church share many of its values.

Like other facets of Ecuadorian culture, religions practiced in Ecuador run the gamut from the mainstream to indigenous religions only found in the country. Evangelical Christians make up over 10 percent of the population, and other religious demographics include Jehovah's Witnesses, Mormons, Buddhists, and Jews. Religious freedom is guaranteed by the constitution of Ecuador.

CATHOLICS

The Catholic Church has exerted tremendous influence over Ecuadorian society for most of the country's history, often in partnership with the government. During the conquest and colonial period, the Spaniards indoctrinated the indigenous peoples with Christianity. In many cases, the Native people adapted the new religion to their own traditional cosmology.

Representatives of the Catholic Church took advantage of this as an intermediate step to conversion; they attempted to eradicate the

Pope Francis during his visit to Ecuador in 2015.

indigenous religions by superimposing Catholic symbols on indigenous religious practices. For instance, the Spaniards constructed Catholic shrines over many of the existing sacred spots of the Incas in the mountains. Many festivals still combine symbols from traditional indigenous beliefs and Catholicism.

Some people devote themselves to Catholicism and may attend Mass on a daily basis. Some Catholics dedicate their lives to the service of a particular saint or make pilgrimages to holy sites around the country. Others simply participate in special ceremonies and rituals, such as baptism and First Communion.

Catholicism so strongly permeates the society, especially in the Sierra, that people often take its influence for granted. They may participate in Catholic rituals, such as godparent relationships, for reasons that are as much cultural as religious. Cultural Catholicism also emphasizes family relationships, social hierarchies, and traditional attitudes about women.

PROTESTANTS AND EVANGELICALS

As in much of South America, Protestantism is growing by leaps and bounds. Ecuador experienced a 5.7 percent growth rate in the percentage of evangelical Protestants from 1960 to 1985—the fourth highest rate of increase in South America. While about 10 percent of the population is affiliated with evangelical Protestant churches, the rapid expansion of Protestant influence, especially among the Native population, has drawn both praise and criticism.

Protestant missionaries in rural areas have built schools, medical clinics, toilets, and other socially beneficial structures. Part of their success in attracting converts from Catholicism (in spite of active opposition from

Travelers to Ecuador used to say that Quito was a city with one hundred churches and only one bathroom. The capital has modernized considerably since the oil boom, but its colonial churches still preside majestically over the impoverished bustle of Old Quito. The Spaniards used local labor to build many churches, which include some of the finest architecture in the Americas. The stunning interior of La Compañía de Jesús is gilded with 7 tons (6.3 metric tons) of gold leaf, and the majestic stone exterior was carved by hand. Construction began in 1605 and took 163 years to complete. Building began on the Church and Monastery of San Francisco in 1534 and took 70 years to finish. The church is the largest colonial structure in Quito and the oldest church on the American continent. There are also beautiful old churches in other large cities, such as Cuenca and Guayaquil, and every small community has at least one church facing the main plaza. The most important churches in the Costa are colonial structures that were damaged by fire and reconstructed.

Small shrines are visible throughout the countryside of the Sierra. The most impressive public sculpture, La Virgen de las Americas, watches over Quito from her pedestal on a hill named El Panecillo. Using symbolism from the Book of Revelation in the Bible, Agustín de la Herrán Matorras's statue of the Virgin Mary wears a crown of stars and stands on a sphere encircled by a serpent, and unlike most statues of the Virgin Mary, it has wings. It was inspired by Bernardo de Legarda's sculpture in the Church and Monastery of San Francisco.

Catholic priests) is due to the fact that they have made special efforts to recognize and respect the indigenous people as equals. Unlike the Catholic Church, Protestant missionaries speak to the Natives in Quechua, offer a Quechua translation of the Bible, and produce radio broadcasts in Quechua. This is a powerful medium to reach a population that had formerly been expected to receive God's message through the language of the whites, who despised them. Many Protestant converts in the Sierra have experienced a renewal of ethnic pride. However, many indigenous people and anthropologists have criticized Protestant missionaries, claiming that their influence leads to the loss of indigenous identity.

Whereas Catholic peasants communally celebrate fiestas in honor of the local patron saint, who is expected to mediate with God on their behalf, the Protestants emphasize an individual relationship with God. The Virgin Mary and the Catholic legion of saints thus lose their importance, eliminating the need for a community fiesta in their honor. When converts to Protestantism stop attending the fiestas, other members of their community charge that they have become antisocial—a serious accusation in a culture that places great emphasis on community relationships and cooperation.

In the past, many Ecuadorians also accused Protestants of trying to "buy" religious influence among the poor by sponsoring social action and giving impoverished communities food and money. Early Protestant missions were responsible for a great deal of acculturation, especially among the indigenous peoples of the Oriente, whose children often forgot their Native language as they grew up in English- or Spanish-speaking boarding schools. It should be noted, however, that a similar process of acculturation had taken place for centuries among the indigenous Serranos who attended Catholic schools. Today, there is a greater emphasis on maintaining indigenous culture, especially indigenous language, alongside Protestant beliefs. Members of the indigenous community are now becoming Protestant pastors.

INDIGENOUS RELIGIONS

The religious beliefs of the indigenous Serranos vary considerably from those of the Oriente Natives. Although most indigenous Serranos are affiliated with the Catholic Church, many have also held on to aspects of their traditional beliefs, blending the two belief systems to form their own worldview.

THE SIERRA Many indigenous Serranos retain vestiges of an ancient belief system. They ascribe qualities such as hot/cold, male/female, weak/strong, and good/evil to natural phenomena. For instance, the Quechua-speaking peoples of the Sierra traditionally call the earth *pachamama*, or "earth mother." This name conveys their affinity to the earth as the source of life. The fertility of the earth is strongly associated with the fertility of women. Many feel that the planting will be especially fertile if sown by a pregnant woman. Indigenous Serranos demonstrate their relationship to the earth by spilling the last drops of alcohol onto the ground at fiestas and other gatherings, in a gesture of offering to pachamama.

The indigenous Serranos see the surrounding Andes Mountains as either male or female, with strong spiritual forces. The sun and the moon are personified with certain negative characteristics. The sun is described as vengeful, striking with illness individuals who defiantly choose not to wear their hat outdoors. Seeds will not germinate if planted during a new moon, and fabrics will fall apart if dyed during the new moon. Rainbows are masculine and live in certain rivers; women who bathe or wash clothes in these rivers may become pregnant.

THE ORIENTE The spiritual beliefs of the indigenous peoples of the Oriente have been strongly influenced by Catholic and Protestant missions during recent decades. Some indigenous peoples have lost their traditional beliefs through Christian education projects, while others have grafted Christian ideas onto their traditional belief systems.

The Shuar, however, have been able to retain their traditional religious beliefs. The spiritual tradition of the Shuar reflects their individualistic quest for power. They believe that humans, plants, animals, spiritual beings, and some inanimate objects have *kakáram* (kah-KAH-rahm), a vital force necessary to survive and to achieve personal goals in the face of opposition. The Shuar believe in an ever-present supernatural world, which humans can see only when in a hallucinogenic state or when dreaming. They identify this

In many communities, people seek out healers, called curanderos (coo-rahn-DAY-rohs), and witches, called brujos (BROO-hos), looking for everything from love potions to a cure for a malnourished baby.

When someone becomes ill, the healer or family classifies the sickness as supernatural, a medical infection, or a humoral imbalance. They seek a doctor's treatment only if they think that the illness is caused by infection. Campesinos generally do not arrive at a Western diagnosis such as malnutrition; they are more likely to attribute sickness to supernatural forces, or the mal *(mahl). However, everyone agrees that illness can be avoided through strength and good nutrition, because the mal preys on weakness.*

Many rural Serranos believe in the same "humoral" theory of disease that once dominated European medicine. In this theory, disease results from an imbalance of four bodily fluids, or humors: blood, black bile, yellow bile, and phlegm. Each of these fluids is defined as "hot," "cold," "wet," or "dry." An excess of any humor upsets the body's equilibrium and causes illness.

Some medical doctors have come to recognize and respect the work of the curanderos; likewise, many curanderos recognize the powers of Western medicine. If either the medical doctor or the healer is unsuccessful in curing a patient, they may recommend that the patient seek attention from the alternative path of medicine. This cooperative relationship is increasingly common in areas with large indigenous populations, as in the Sierra and the Oriente.

Other private hospitals take cooperation a step further by offering Western medical interventions and folk healing under the same roof. These private hospitals see the benefit of working together to provide patients with a range of treatments. The Alternative Andean Hospital is one such facility. The hospital is located in Riobamba and has a folk healer on staff.

It seems that this kind of collaboration is here to stay. The 2008 constitution includes a clause that "traditional medical practices" are a fundamental right of "communities, peoples, and nations."

world as the "real world," with which they must become familiar in order to learn the true nature of the universe and to acquire the tools to protect themselves in the waking world. Any adult man or woman may become a shaman, one who is able to cross over to the supernatural world. Most of the indigenous people of the Oriente are egalitarian in their social order, and anyone with sufficient innate power can become a shaman through apprenticeship for several years.

The Shuar believe that the power of knowledge grows stronger with its distance from local sources. Indeed, a Shuar seeks to obtain knowledge from outside sources, whether from indigenous Serranos, whites, or other outsiders.

In 2006, Ecuador competed in the World Cup; a Shuar shaman ritually prepared the arena.

A representation
of the *duende*.

They count their ability to cross cultural boundaries through language and dress as an additional sign of strength.

A MELTING POT OF BELIEFS

Many campesinos combine traditional beliefs, Catholic teachings, and medieval Spanish beliefs. They believe that many spirits and supernatural forces inhabit and threaten their world and may strike people who are vulnerable. The *duende* (DWEN-day) is an elflike being with large eyes and a huge hat that likes to prey on large-eyed children with abundant hair. The *huacaisiqui* (hwa-kai-SEE-kee) are spirits of aborted or abandoned infants who steal babies' souls. Campesinos may also believe in spirits of the mountain mist, rainbows, and other natural phenomena.

The in-between periods of dawn and dusk and the hours of noon and midnight appear as cracks through which supernatural spirits and forces can enter or escape the human world. Noon and midnight are considered to be dangerous times to be abroad because of their ambiguity: they are neither morning nor afternoon, neither night nor morning.

This worldview inspires the aloof behavior that often characterizes the highland indigenous peoples. Since encounters with strangers can lead to supernatural attacks, they try to remain in familiar company. Among the Saraguros, women regard the outside world as threatening, while the home serves as a refuge from illness and danger.

Afro-Ecuadorians in Esmeraldas also have a wealth of spiritual beliefs, many from Africa. The *tunda*, for example, is a malevolent water creature and a child of the devil. She appears as a deformed woman with huge lips and a clubfoot. Unable to bear children, she steals them. The Esmeraldeños protect their children by not letting them go out without protective dogs.

INTERNET LINKS

www.bbc.com/news/world-latin-america-18483584
In this article, the BBC reports on the Alternative Andean Hospital in Ecuador, which treats patients with a blend of indigenous medicine and Western medicine.

www.pewforum.org/2015/04/02/religious-projection-table
The Pew Research Center predicts the religious makeup of countries around the world, including Ecuador, through 2050.

www.state.gov/j/drl/rls/irf/religiousfreedom/index.htm?year=2014 &dlid=238542#wrapper
The US Department of State's "International Religious Freedom Report: Ecuador (2014)" records instances of religious discrimination, discusses demographics, and notes discussions between US and Ecuadorian officials about maintaining religious freedom.

LANGUAGE

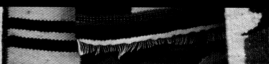

Unlike most nations, Ecuador has scores of written and spoken languages.

9

I N A BID TO FOSTER INCLUSIVITY, Ecuador's most recent constitution made two indigenous languages, Kichwa and Shuar, "official languages for intercultural ties" in 2008. Spanish remains the official language of Ecuador in all administrative matters, but the constitutional inclusion of Kichwa and Shuar points to language's role in Ecuadorian identity. Over twenty languages are spoken in Ecuador, and linguists who study indigenous languages flock to the country.

English is one of the many languages spoken in Ecuador. Educated Ecuadorians use English when conducting business. Speaking English is seen as a status symbol, so Ecuadorians are eager to learn the language.

INDIGENOUS LANGUAGES

Many indigenous people throughout the Sierra and the Oriente speak Quechua. The unrelated Shuar language spreads nearly as far in the Oriente as Quechua does. Smaller language groupings in the Oriente include Cofán, Siona-Secoya, Waorani, and Zaparoan.

None of the indigenous peoples had a written language prior to the Spanish conquest, nor do any of their languages have their own indigenous alphabet. Outsiders, primarily missionaries, have phonetically

This map shows the areas where Quechua is spoken, with each color representing a different dialect.

transcribed their languages into either English or Spanish. Because of the various alphabets that have been devised for the languages, many words can be spelled different ways. For instance, the name by which the people who used to be called Aucas identify themselves can be spelled Waorani (in English) or Huarani (in Spanish).

Indigenous organizations have recently begun to demand official recognition of their native languages but have achieved only minor success. In addition to the recognition of their languages in the 2008 constitution, they have succeeded in obtaining bilingual education in many schools, which will help stop the erosion of their languages among the younger generations. Nonetheless, although the minister of education has been willing to permit bilingual education in the schools, he has prohibited the actual substitution of any indigenous language for Spanish-language instruction, thus indicating the government's unwillingness to recognize a second official language.

The Incas adopted Quechua as their language because it was already widespread within and beyond the borders of their empire. Today, Quechua is spoken by around 13 million people from Colombia to Argentina, making it the most commonly spoken indigenous language in the Americas. In reality, Quechua consists of multiple dialects, not all of which are mutually intelligible.

Oriente Kichwa cultures share other characteristics in addition to their language, such as agricultural proficiency, hunting and fishing techniques, and a spiritual perception of the environment.

The second language family in the Oriente, next to Quechua, is Shuar. The Shuar share their language, as well as cultural characteristics, with several Amazonian peoples of Peru.

SPANISH

When the Spaniards first came to the Americas, they introduced Spanish as the common language. During the colonial period, various Creole languages also developed, some of which are still spoken today in parts of Ecuador. For example, some people in the Costa region speak a Creole Spanish. Quechua, however, remained relatively unchanged by the introduction of Spanish. The two languages borrowed words from each other and influenced each other's syntax only to a minor extent.

Regional differences in spoken Spanish are notable. Serranos speak sixteenth-century Andalusian, while Costeños tend to swallow the last syllable of most words and eliminate most of the s sounds. In Guayaquil, the phrase *más o menos* (mahs oh MAY-nohs) ends up sounding like "maomay." This speech pattern is the main Costeño characteristic.

Today, only the most isolated Ecuadorians of the high Sierra region or of the deep jungles of the Oriente region do not speak or understand Spanish. Many indigenous peoples are bilingual and use Spanish when speaking to people from other language groups.

DEMONSTRATING COURTESY

Ecuadorians prize gestures of courtesy, particularly in the Sierra. Even when discussing business, Ecuadorians will always spend at least a minute of conversation chatting graciously before initiating the substance of the conversation. They often regard people from the United States as rude and abrupt, because North Americans jump right into a conversation without engaging in the requisite preliminary courtesies. Even conversations between strangers begin with the cordial greeting: "Buenos días, ¿Cómo está?" ("Good day, how are you?")

Another custom of courtesy among Ecuadorians, especially in the Sierra, is to politely pretend agreement regardless of circumstances or true feelings. Part of the Serrano system of courtesy is making extravagant promises without the expectation of fulfilling them. Also, if asked a question about something of which they have no knowledge, they will often dissemble and say anything to hide the fact that they do not know. This well-intended behavior provides the basis for the disapproval that Costeños often express toward Serranos, whom they accuse of being false and superficial.

Not accounting for regional and clan variations in slang, when Ecuadorians want to say that something is fun or especially good, they say

SAVING DYING LANGUAGES

Due to changing lifestyles and demographics, there are twelve indigenous languages in Ecuador that are classified as endangered. These languages have UNESCO ratings ranging from "definitely endangered" to "critically endangered." UNESCO tracks the health of languages around the world. The UNESCO website includes an "Interactive Atlas of the World's Languages in Danger," which features information like the geographic area in which a language is spoken, the language's alternate names, and the number of language speakers. According to this incredible resource, two languages in Ecuador—Tetete and Andoa—have already gone extinct.

Organizations and language activists work together to ensure the survival of indigenous languages. The National Geographic Society has the Enduring Voices project, which aims to document the linguistic structure of endangered languages. A linguistic anthropologist spearheaded a South American "language expedition" in 2011 through Enduring Voices. Some formal programs at  *universities share the mission of keeping languages alive. The University of Cuenca in Ecuador offers courses in Quechua, for example.*

it is chevere (CHAY-ver-ay). When they want to describe something as being fierce, they use the word *bravo* (brah-voh).

GREETINGS AND GESTURES

Like most South Americans, many Ecuadorians greet and say goodbye with a single kiss on the cheek. Female friends greet each other with a kiss, as do male and female acquaintances, except when conducting business. Men do not kiss other men; rather, they shake hands with male acquaintances and hug close friends. Between men and women, and among women, a single meeting is enough of a basis to greet each other with a kiss. This is a courtesy performed only between acquaintances of the same social class, however.

Traditionally, the indigenous peoples were conditioned to greet their social superiors with deference, keeping their eyes cast down and removing their hats. Today, young Native people expect to be treated with the same respect as everyone else. Within indigenous communities, the most common way to greet people is with a handshake, and both men and women shake hands. The practice of kissing cheeks has not been widely adopted in these communities.

A form of sexism that occurs daily in communication between men and women is the macho hissing at women on the street. Depending on their social class and education, men may hiss at women passersby, making a sound by pressing their tongue to the back of their teeth. Many women choose to ignore this behavior instead of engaging in a confrontation, although many show discreet irritation when such an action occurs.

INTERNET LINKS

www.britannica.com/topic/South-American-Indian-languages
The *Encyclopedia Britannica* gives background information about South American indigenous languages.

www.duolingo.com/course/es/en/Learn-Spanish-Online
Find free online Spanish lessons on this website.

www.omniglot.com/writing/quechua.htm
Explore an overview of the Quechua language, sample text, pronunciation tips, and useful links on Omniglot's "Quechua" page.

ARTS

Museums across Ecuador feature ancient and modern art.

10

A RT IN ECUADOR RANGES FROM traditional handicrafts to modern paintings by masters like Oswaldo Guayasamín. For centuries, indigenous peoples have passed down skills like making ceramics and creating intricate weavings. Beyond art that can be worn or used, Ecuadorians are known for groundbreaking novels, music, architecture, and dance.

The Valdivia culture's painted ceramics have influenced several modern Ecuadorian painters.

Oswaldo Guayasamín's *El Descubriento del Amazonas.*

These paintings are in the style of the Quito School.

These creative works are celebrated in Ecuador. Every two years, the Eugenio Espejo Prize is awarded to achievers in literature, art, culture, and science. The award is overseen by the National Council of Culture, which creates a list of nominees. The president of Ecuador picks the recipients from this list.

PAINTING

Ecuador boasts a long history of well-developed painting styles. The two most notable artistic trends include the colonial Quito School and the twentieth-century school of *indigenismo* (in-dee-hain-EES-mo). The Quito School developed during the colonial period as a style based on religious subjects, such as the Virgin Mary, the Catholic saints, and Christ. Indigenismo is a contemporary movement that uses indigenous subject matter. It has influenced both the visual and literary arts.

THE QUITO SCHOOL The Spaniards brought to the Americas their European conceptions of art, which often revolved around Catholic religious themes. Beginning in the sixteenth century, they started training local indigenous artists to produce sculptures, paintings, and gold works with religious themes. This combination of Spanish religious concepts executed by indigenous artists developed into the Quito School of art, which lasted throughout the colonial period and well after independence.

The Quito School also influenced architecture. Quito's colonial churches are characterized by an almost overwhelming degree of ornamentation. Many churches are crowded with paintings and sculptures from the Quito School. A particularly common subject in both media is an anguished Christ on the cross, his wounds appearing to ooze realistic blood. The paintings have an imposing presence with their enormous size and dark, solemn tone.

INDIGENISMO The twentieth century brought the rise of indigenismo, which is characterized more by its subject matter than by a common artistic style. The unifying theme is the denunciation of the oppression of Ecuador's indigenous peoples. Painting styles range from realism to impressionism, cubism, and surrealism. The most famous painters of this school include Eduardo Kingman, Camilo Egas, and Oswaldo Guayasamín.

Camilo Egas's *Trabajadores sin hogar.*

Eduardo Kingman (1913—1997) has been described as the prototypical *indigenista* (in-dee-hain-EES-ta). His work since the 1930s consisted of murals, oil paintings, and book illustrations that experiment with color and depict subjects of oppression. Kingman's oil paintings display semi-abstract human images with heavy facial features and huge, distorted hands.

The early works of Camilo Egas (1889—1962) are surrealist in style. In the 1950s, he switched to realism and produced paintings that conveyed a sense of dignity rather than of misery. From the late 1950s until his death in 1962, Egas switched to abstract expressionism.

Oswaldo Guayasamín (1919—1999) is closely identified with modern art in Ecuador. His father was a Native person whose heritage greatly influenced Guayasamín's work. Guayasamín is most commonly associated with his cubist paintings of tortured and oppressed indigenous peoples. The tone of suffering in these representations of Natives is influenced by the religious artwork of the Quito School. He often used enormous canvases, almost overwhelming the viewer with life-sized, graphic images of misery.

CONTEMPORARY PAINTING Contemporary painters have moved away from indigenismo to the portrayal of more personalized themes. Ramiro Jácome of Quito started out in the 1970s painting in a neo-figurative style. In the early 1980s, he created a series of abstract oil paintings characterized

The Capilla del Hombre Museum honors Guayasamín's art.

by rich, deep colors. Before his death in 2001, he returned to figurative works that portray aspects of Ecuadorian daily life. Jácome is still considered to be the most important Ecuadorian neo-figurative painter. Other Ecuadorian artists of note include Jaime Romero and Washington Iza.

LITERATURE

Ecuador has produced many fine writers, most significantly during the twentieth century. Although novels, poetry, and essays are common, the most important literary form is the short story. Very few women writers are included in the lists of Ecuador's finest, although a few have achieved notice in recent decades. One such example is Alicia Yánez Cossío (1929–). In several novels since the 1970s, she has explored the position of women in Ecuadorian society, often with great use of satire.

One of the most notable writers of the nineteenth century was Juan Montalvo (1832–1889), a prolific essayist who wrote about contemporary politics and was a strong critic of dictators such as Gabriel García Moreno. His best-known work is the 1882 compilation of essays *Siete Tratados* (Seven Treatises), which includes a comparison of the revolutionary heroes Simón Bolívar and George Washington.

One of the most significant Ecuadorian writers of the twentieth century was Jorge Icaza (1906–1978), who authored the first indigenista novel in South America. *Huasipungo* (1934) brutally depicts the oppression of indigenous campesinos by the hacienda, or farm, owners, who seize their communal lands and massacre those who protest. The novel wrenchingly portrays how the Natives are trapped in their suffering by the rest of society, especially by the landowners, the Catholic Church, and the military. In 1974, the novel was translated into English as *The Villagers*. Icaza was also known as a playwright, an actor, and a writer of short stories.

Many significant authors have come from the Costa, including the "Guayaquil Group," whose writing explored life among the *montuvios*, people of mixed black, indigenous, and white ancestry. Guayaquil native José Antonio Campos (1868—1939) established himself as a pioneer in early twentieth-century Ecuadorian literature.

DANCE

Although in mainstream Ecuadorian culture dance is primarily a form of entertainment, certain traditional dances are performed during festivals. During Corpus Christi, for instance, many people in the areas surrounding Quito have traditionally danced the *yumbo* (YOOM-boh), where they dress in plumed costumes and stop traffic with mock ambushes. Some people still perform a Spanish folkloric dance called the *cueca* (KWAY-kah), in which couples dance together holding handkerchiefs, although it is primarily danced at festivals.

At weddings and parties, people dance the *cumbia* (KOOM-bya) and the *sanjuanito* (sahn-hwa-NEE-toh) to music that is played by traditional musicians or by bands with amplified instruments. Indigenous groups have a variety of dances to celebrate courtship and other rituals. Many indigenous dances involve rings of couples with a play of hats or handkerchiefs.

Traditional dance is an important part of celebrating festivals.

MUSIC

Ecuadorians generally love music—especially dance music, such as the Caribbean salsa or merengue and the Colombian cumbia. Cumbia is very popular on the coast and is often identified as Costeño music. Instruments such as trumpets, tubas, trombones, clarinets, cymbals, and French horns are often played for small-town fiestas.

Ecuador established a national conservatory of music over 115 years ago. Many classical artists, such as Domenico Brescia, a native of Italy who has taught in Ecuador for many years (*Ecuadoran Symphony*), and Segundo Luis

The Ecuador Children's Symphony Orchestra during a concert in Quito.

Moreno (*Three Ecuadorian Suites*), have included indigenous melodies in their compositions. Luis Humberto Salgado composed a symphonic suite entitled *Atahualpa* that utilizes indigenous elements.

SHUAR MUSIC Shuar music is based on a three-note scale. The Shuar sing three types of songs, or *nampesmas*: love songs, gardening songs, and social or public songs. They used to sing a fourth type, war songs, until the missionaries came. Women sing most often and teach nampesmas to their daughters, but men can sing also. Women are not allowed to play instruments, however. Men play a flute, violin, or musical bow.

Nampesmas do not include music played for ceremonial purposes, such as a shaman's curing ceremonies. Ritual music uses different instruments, such as the large slit drum, the two-headed drum, and the seed or shell rattle belts.

ANDEAN MUSIC Traditional Andean music is based on a five-note scale and uses three basic types of instruments: wind, percussion, and rattles and bells. The Spaniards introduced string instruments, which were quickly adopted. The combination of these instruments with the pentatonic scale produces a hauntingly breathy sound.

Wind instruments include flutes, panpipes, and conch shells. The *quena* (KAY-nah) is a notched bamboo flute that was once made from the leg bones of a condor. Percussion instruments include drums called *bombos*. The musicians also use bells, or *campañas* (cahm-PAH-nyahs), and various rattles, including gourd rattles, known as maracas. The panpipe, or *rondador* (rohn-dah-DOHR), is fashioned of varying lengths and diameters of either cane or bamboo pipes tied together in a long row.

The Spaniards introduced string instruments such as the guitar, violin, and mandolin. Ecuadorian musicians adopted the *charanga* (cha-RAHN-gah) and the Andean harp. The small charanga originated in Bolivia and is made traditionally from the shell of an armadillo. More recently, Andean musicians have incorporated the accordion and the harmonica into their instrumentation.

A shaman plays a traditional instrument called a Jew's harp.

The Panama hat, or sombrero de paja *(sohm-BRAY-roh day PAH-ha), is an indigenous product of Ecuador. It became known as the Panama hat because it passed through Panama on its way to the United States.*

Panama hats are woven from thin toquilla *(toh-KEE-ya) straw, which grows on bushes in the coastal lowlands.* Pajeros *(pah-HAY-rohs), or straw cutters, harvest the toquilla straw, then transport it to warehouses in Guayaquil. It is then shipped to straw markets in Cuenca and other weaving centers. Every week, tens of thousands of campesinos come from the countryside around Cuenca and parts of the Costa to the nearest weaving center. They carefully choose the lengths of straw for a single hat, the quality of which will determine their weekly income. Most weavers are women who learned the craft at a young age from their mothers as a means of supplementing the family income.*

Although most of the weavers work in the southern Sierra, the finest hats are made in Montecristi and Jipijapa, near the coast. Both cities are centuries-old indigenous communities, although they are now part mestizo and white. Panama hats come in all qualities, from coarsely woven to "superfine." The hats of Montecristi are so finely woven they can hold water. The first 6 inches (15.2 cm) can take as long as fifteen days to make, while the rest of the crown may take three weeks. Six or more coarsely woven hats can be finished in one week.

TEXTILES

The indigenous peoples of the Otavalo area, north of Quito, have distinguished themselves by their weaving for centuries. The traditional weaving tool was a backstrap loom, which some people still use. The Spaniards introduced the treadle loom, the spinning wheel, hand carders, wool, and silk, and some people now use electric looms and synthetic fibers. In 1917, local weavers began to produce fine fabrics to compete with British imports, and the Otavalo weavers entered the cash economy.

OTAVALO MARKET

Arts and handicrafts are big business in Ecuador. Markets in cities around the country cater to tourists with their wares, but many say that the market in Otavalo is the most important, citing the history behind the bazaar. The craftspeople of Otavalo can trace the tradition of weaving textiles back to their Inca ancestors, and the Otavalo Market has existed since even before the Incas! The market features jewelry, purses, pan flutes, and traditional food.

The weavers obtain their wool locally from sheep and llamas, and occasionally from alpacas in Peru. Many Otavalo front doors open into a family workshop within the home. Men traditionally do the weaving, although many women weave also.

INTERNET LINKS

www.bbc.com/travel/story/20131230-otavalo-the-land-of-andean-artistry
The BBC takes a closer look at the Otavalo Market.

www.frommers.com/destinations/ecuador/632201
Frommer's provides a brief history of Ecuadorian art and architecture.

www.npr.org/sections/altlatino/2013/09/30/227834004/cumbia-the-musical-backbone-of-latin-america
NPR talks to musicians and traces the spread of cumbia in "Cumbia: The Musical Backbone of Latin America." The story includes embedded music videos from nine artists.

LEISURE

Soccer is a wildly popular sport in Ecuador. Here, an Ecuador player (*left*) goes for a header against a Mexico player (*right*) during the 2015 Copa América in Chile.

11

T HE FACE OF LEISURE IN ECUADOR IS changing, and it's because of a surprising source. The 2011 referendum to the constitution saw the end of gambling, which was previously a popular pastime in the nation. The referendum also affected traditions like bullfighting and cockfighting, though these events were not criminalized outright.

The colonial Spanish ethos of leisure, and the socioeconomic system that has for so long supported it, is revealed in an Ecuadorian saying: "The clever one lives off the foolish, and the foolish lives off his labor."

Despite new legislation, many aspects of leisure in Ecuador remain the same. Ecuadorians value their free time and often spend hours outside of work with family and friends. Young Ecuadorians in cities enjoy nights out on the town, and Ecuadorians with resources travel domestically and internationally.

DOWN TIME

For most Ecuadorians, time off centers around the numerous holidays. During the normal course of the week, however, most people find time to relax by socializing with family and friends. On Sunday, people gather after church in the town plaza. Men may attend a cockfight. In Quito and Ibarra, playing glove ball is very popular on Sunday afternoons. There are soccer matches almost every weekend at the local stadium or soccer field.

In the evening, families may go out or stay home. In middle- and upper-class homes, the family watches television in the parents' bedroom. In small towns and rural areas, neighbors may gather at a

Guayaquil (pictured here) is known for its nightlife.

friend's house to listen to the radio or watch television. Storytelling used to be very popular in places such as Esmeraldas and the Oriente, but the custom is dying out due to the prevalence of television and radio.

For the urban middle and upper class, evening is the time to dress up and go out dancing, to the theater, to hear a concert, or simply to visit friends. Young Ecuadorians especially like to go out in groups to discotheques, where they can dance to salsa, cumbia, or folk music. They might also go to a movie theater, where they can watch films from the United States, Europe, Mexico, or Argentina.

Small towns tend to offer little more than the local cinema as entertainment, except during the town's fiesta day, when the town celebrates with music, dancing, food, games, and parades.

BULLFIGHTS

Historically, bullfighting has been a popular event in Ecuador, especially in the Sierra. Bullfighting dates back to eighteenth-century Spain. In its ritualized brutality, bullfighting exalts the heroic virtues of machismo: braided silk suits and spears, graceful pomp and spurting blood, camaraderie and individual heroism. The audience praises the accomplished bullfighter, or *torero* (toh-RAY-roh), with wild enthusiasm and cascading flowers, but boos and heckles the torero who botches the job. The bulls are carefully bred and selected from reputable haciendas in Ecuador. Spectators love to see a bravo bull—aggressive, but dignified and stately. Indeed, the bull represents heroism and machismo as well.

After allowing the bull to circle the ring a few times, a team of *picadores* (pee-kah-DOH-rays), mounted on padded and blindfolded horses, approach the bull. Drawing his attention to them, they quickly close in on the animal and cast small, colorfully decorated spears into the bull's upper back, making the blood run down his body. This enrages the bull and the procedure is repeated until the bull is running and snorting around the ring with four to six of the bright *picos* (PEE-kohs) in his massive shoulders.

Then the *matador* (MAH-tah-dor), the torero who kills the bull, makes his entrance. He walks out into the bullring, bows to the audience, to the judges, and to the bull, then presents his scarlet cape. He waves it in front of the bull a few times, drawing the animal's rage toward him and allowing the bull to pass under the cape. The matador has to be extremely quick and graceful in stepping aside to avoid being gored by the bull's horns. When the relationship has been established, the matador and the bull face off. The bull charges him once more—and if the matador is skilled or lucky enough, he plunges his sword through the animal's spine, killing it with a single thrust.

A bullfight in Quito in 2010.

Today in Ecuador, bullfighting is still an important tradition, though the 2011 referendum to the constitution has outlawed killing animals in public during sporting events in towns that voted "yes" to the proposition. In the towns that voted "yes," either the bull is not killed or it is taken into a barn (out of public view) to be killed at the end of the match. Quito voted "yes" on this bullfighting proposition, which effectively ended the Quito bullfighting festival. The Quito bullfight celebrated the founding of the city and hosted one of its twice-yearly bullfight competitions during the first week of December. During the Quito Day celebrations, Ecuadorian toreros competed with international bullfighters in a series of ten bullfights. The final Quito bullfighting festival was held in 2011.

COCKFIGHTS

Cockfighting is also popular all over Ecuador, and most towns have a cockfighting coliseum. Cockfighting is a sport of ancient origins, in which the owners of the gamecocks, or *gallos* (GAH-yohs), place their birds in a circular

Though Ecuadorian moviegoers usually watch English-language films, the tide is starting to change in favor of homegrown films. According to the BBC in 2012, "National productions have gone up by 300% … making cinema the most dynamic cultural sector in the country." Some productions have found Ecuador to be a great place to shoot, including 2004's Maria Full of Grace, *which filmed in two locations in the country and received widespread critical acclaim.*

ring about 20 feet (6 m) in diameter and make them fight each other. Their handlers equip the birds with metal or bone spurs, averaging about 1.5 inches (4 cm) in length, to increase their ability to injure the other birds in the ring.

After placing the artificial spur over the natural spur of the gamecock, the handlers "set" the birds into the ring at the same time. Infuriated at the proximity of the opponent, each bird runs and jumps, trying to spur and wound the other in the eyes or chest. If one refuses to fight, the handler puts it breast to breast with the other. If it still refuses, the judge rules that it has quit, and the fight ends.

The 2011 referendum to the constitution that aimed to outlaw the killing of animals for sport has surprisingly not affected cockfighting. President Correa determined that the intention of a cockfight is not the death of the bird. Therefore, cockfighting is legal as long as the birds do not fight to the death.

ATHLETIC EVENTS

Soccer, or *fútbol* (FOOT-bohl), is the national game and is played at all levels in the Costa and in the Sierra. Ecuador's national team competes internationally, while other teams—professional and amateur—play throughout the country, either in formal matches or informally on Sunday afternoons.

Every match at any level, especially the World Cup, generates great excitement among spectators. Streets empty as fans crowd the stadiums for local and national games, and people all over the country gather around their radios and television sets. If their team wins, they pour out onto the streets and celebrate.

The second most popular game is basketball, and Ecuadorians also enjoy playing volleyball. Tennis became popular in the early 1990s, partly due to the success of Ecuadorian tennis player Andrés Gómez, who won the US Open in Men's Doubles in 1986 and the French Open in 1990.

Another very popular game in Ibarra and Quito is glove ball, or *pelota de guante* (pay-LOH-tah day HWAN-tay), which is played almost exclusively in Ecuador. The players gather on Sunday afternoons. They wear gloves attached to a round, flat wooden paddle with spikes. The players use them to hit a rubber ball back and forth to each other.

Children play a game of soccer before their school day.

INTERNET LINKS

www.bbc.co.uk/sport/football/teams/ecuador
The BBC provides up-to-date news about Ecuador's soccer team.

www.si.com/planet-futbol/2015/06/21/colombia-ecuador-womens-world-cupx
This *Sports Illustrated* article looks at Ecuador's "increasing investment in women's soccer."

FESTIVALS

Carnival is celebrated across Ecuador. Here, a young woman wears a traditional costume while dancing during a Carnival parade.

FESTIVALS ARE CELEBRATED ALL over Ecuador—in both small towns and big cities. These festivals are often in honor of Catholic holidays, though many pay tribute to indigenous beliefs or mark an important moment in a town's history. Ecuadorians gather together for music and revelry. Food and drink are a big part of the fun.

Festivals in Ecuador are known for being colorful and over-the-top. Carnival—the equivalent of Mardi Gras in the United States—is celebrated for a full week or more and ushers in Lent. Water fights are unique features of Carnival in Ecuador—not even innocent bystanders are safe from water balloons, buckets of water, and water guns! In some cities, a water attack is finished with a bucket of flour, which results in a sticky situation.

PATRON SAINTS' DAYS

Ecuador observes many religious holidays, both nationally and locally. Each town has a patron saint, in whose honor a special day is celebrated each year. Some of the local patron saints' days have become famous throughout Ecuador for their colorful festivities, which usually begin the night before the actual day of observance. Although the holidays were originally introduced by the Catholic Church, they are not somber affairs. Rather patron saints' days are often characterized by great extravagance.

Fanesca soup

In the Otavalo area, the festival of San Juan Bautista, or Saint John the Baptist, most likely replaced the indigenous celebration of the summer solstice and is on June 24. (The celebration of the ancient Festival of the Sun, Inti Raymi, is being revived in Ecuador after being suppressed during the Spanish period.) Today, the Catholic fiesta lasts nearly a week and is filled with costumes, dancing, and music. The fiesta music is rhythmic, often repeating a single refrain over and over again, with slight variations.

The Day of Saint John the Baptist is a festival for the men, who dress up in an astounding variety of costumes, including satirized characters with blonde wigs, wide sombreros, and women. Each night, groups of musicians and dancers move from house to house, stamping in a circle and reversing direction suddenly. A custom that seems connected to pachamama rituals in Bolivia and Peru consists of throwing rocks at the chapels dedicated to Saint John the Baptist.

Another festival in Imbabura Province, and especially in Cotacachi, is the Day of Saints Peter and Paul. While John the Baptist is the patron saint for the Otavaleños, Peter is the patron saint for the other group of Native people in Imbabura Province. On June 29, hundreds of people descend on the town of Cayambe, where the patron saint is also Peter. The Day of Saint John the Baptist and the Day of Saints Peter and Paul are sometimes celebrated together for a week or more.

EASTER TRADITIONS

As one of the most important holidays on the Catholic Church calendar, Easter presents an occasion for great celebration. It is preceded by Holy Week, and in many towns, costumed worshippers observe Good Friday two days before Easter by reenacting the procession of Christ carrying the cross. Religious processions also take place on Holy Saturday and Easter Sunday.

On Easter Sunday, after Mass, many devout families gather for a feast consisting of a traditional Ecuadorian soup called *fanesca* (fahn-AYS-kah). Fanesca combines ingredients from the lowlands and from the highlands, including onions, peanuts, fish, rice, squash, broad beans, lupine, corn, lentils, beans, peas, and *melloco* (may-YOH-koh), a highland tuber.

EL DÍA DE LOS DIFUNTOS

El Día de los Difuntos (dee-FOON-tohs), the Day of the Deceased, is an occasion observed on November 2, the day after All Saints' Day. Many Ecuadorian families visit the cemeteries on the Day of the Deceased in remembrance of their loved ones, and they bring flowers to decorate the graves.

Cleaning graves is part of marking the Day of the Deceased.

The birthday of Venezuelan Simón Bolívar is a national holiday in Ecuador. Bolívar's leadership in military campaigns against the Spanish in 1813 earned him the nickname El Libertador (the Liberator) across South America, and his role as a liberator was eventually honored in a lasting way: the country of Bolivia is named after him.

On July 24, Ecuadorians mark the birthday of Simón Bolívar ("El Natalicio de Simón Bolívar" in Spanish) with military parades, brass bands, food, and even historical reenactments. The official government website of Ecuador notes that the day is celebrated virtually around the world with special hashtags commemorating Bolívar. For those celebrating in Ecuador, the day is a bank holiday, so the whole nation enjoys a day off from work.

CORPUS CHRISTI

This holiday is usually observed on the Thursday after Trinity Sunday, in honor of the Eucharist. Although celebrated in many parts of Ecuador, it is only considered a major fiesta among certain indigenous groups in the central Sierra.

In some communities, traditional dancers with ornate headdresses and embroidered costumes celebrate with music and dance. In Salasaca, the Natives wear plaster masks, and ribbons and feathers on their hats, and they dance along the streets to the next town.

CHRISTMAS

Christmas is a religious holiday in Ecuador. One traditional custom, especially in Cuenca, is the *Pase del Niño* (PAH-say del NEEN-yoh), or the presentation of the Christ child. Especially in the smaller towns and villages, people carry statues of the baby Jesus to the local church, walking in a procession accompanied by musicians and costumed children who represent the nativity. The priest blesses the statues in a special Mass, after which the families take them back to their household crèches. Christmas trees have become more popular in recent years, but Ecuadorians lavish much more attention on their nativity scenes, which can be quite elaborate.

Many Ecuadorians start celebrating Christmas at the beginning of December. Families hold *novenas* (noh-BAY-nahs) in the days preceding Christmas. They gather at a different family member's house each evening for prayers and singing. The family concludes the evening's devotions with a party with lots of food and alcohol.

On Christmas Eve, everyone attends the midnight Mass, after which they return home to eat and drink the night away. The traditional Christmas drink is *canelazo* (cah-nay-LAH-soh), made from hot water, sugarcane alcohol, lemon, and cinnamon. People exchange gifts on Christmas Day, and the extended family again assembles for another feast.

The Christmas season concludes on January 6 with the Festival of the Three Kings, also known as Epiphany. Because Epiphany involves presents, toys, and candy, this holiday is primarily for children.

THE INDIGENOUS FIESTA SYSTEM

For centuries, the indigenous peoples of the Sierra have participated in a formalized fiesta system where one person from the group is chosen each year to host the patron saint's celebration.

Young men first assume a particular menial task known as a *cargo* (KAR-goh), or burden. For instance, they might have to clean the church or serve as the night watchman. By the time they reach adulthood, their cargo would have increased to the level of being responsible for organizing and carrying out the costly festival for the village's patron saint. As a man fulfills his religious obligations, he gains prestige and disposes of his wealth. The host of the fiesta also serves on the town council for the year.

It was once believed that the indigenous fiesta system served to ensure that no one individual became significantly richer than everyone else in the community. Since the 1964 land reform, however, this system has become less common, and the cost of holding the fiesta is often paid for through collections and contributions from the members of the community.

NEW YEAR'S EVE

On the last night of the year, December 31, Ecuadorians say good-bye to El Año Viejo (the old year) and greet El Año Nuevo (the new year). They light bonfires and stuff old clothes to make life-sized puppets. The puppets are called *los viejos* (vee-AY-hos) and symbolize the old year; sometimes, they are fashioned humorously to represent political figures. Especially in Guayaquil and Esmeraldas, the people display los viejos on the main streets of the city and burn them in the bonfires at midnight.

FOUNDING DAYS

People in Guayaquil, Quito, and Cuenca all go wild celebrating the founding of their cities. They have parades, fireworks, art shows, and beauty pageants.

Ecuadorians burning puppets (*los viejos*) on New Year's Eve.

As always, there is plenty of music and dancing in the streets, combined with lots of eating and drinking.

These festivals are remarkable for the intensity with which the citizens participate in the events. Open-air concerts are attended by thousands of people, who pack themselves onto the streets so tightly that they can hardly move.

Guayaquil combines the celebration for the Founding of Guayaquil (July 25) with that for Simón Bolívar's birthday (July 24); festivities sometimes begin even a few days earlier. The Founding of Cuenca (November 3) is celebrated in conjunction with All Saints' Day and the Day of the Deceased (November 1—2), which makes this a particularly spectacular festival for the city.

INTERNET LINKS

www.ecuador.com/events
Ecuador.com maintains a list of upcoming holidays and festivals.

internationalliving.com/2013/11/five-great-traditional-festivals-ecuador
International Living highlights memorable festivals in a post called "Five Great Traditional Festivals in Ecuador."

www.timeanddate.com/holidays/ecuador
This website gives a listing of holidays observed in Ecuador.

FOOD

Outdoor cafés in Quito serve coffee in style.

ECUADORIAN FOOD IS NOT AS SPICY as the cuisine of its Latin American neighbors. Raw ingredients like potatoes, fruits, beans, and seafood pack enough flavor on their own. Ecuadorian farmers are able to raise this impressive range of crops thanks to a high percentage of arable and pasture land. In fact, nearly 30 percent of the country's land is used for agriculture.

One of the most influential legacies of the Spanish conquest of the Americas was the wide variety of foods they took back to Europe. The potato, for instance, completely changed the basic diet of many European societies.

Quinoa is an ancient grain that has grown in Ecuador for thousands of years.

Ecuador has a long tradition of growing staple grains. Indigenous peoples in the Andes first raised quinoa (a highland grain) around four thousand years ago. Today the Ecuadorian diet is characterized by its reliance on meats, seafood, and starches.

MEALS

Ecuadorians favor a lot of fried foods, and they eat rice or potatoes with almost every meal, sometimes together. White rice is usually served plain and sticky but is sometimes prepared as a combination dish with chicken or beef. Ecuadorian cuisine makes heavy use of cilantro, an herb similar to parsley.

Some traditional dishes include *humitas* (oo-MEE-tahs), which are sweet corn tamales; empanadas, which are meat-filled pastries; *choclos* (CHOH-clohs), which are ears of corn toasted in fat; *lechón* (lay-CHOHN), or suckling pig; and *cuy* (KWEE), or guinea pig.

Humitas

Ecuadorian families eat most of their meals together, except on occasions when one or more of the family members are unable to return home from work or school for the midday meal. Most middle- and upper-class families have a maid who either lives in the house or comes to work daily. She prepares all the meals, often with instructions for the menu from the mother of the household.

Ecuadorians eat a light breakfast, especially in the highlands, where the atmosphere is so thin that they do not like to start the day with a "heavy stomach." Breakfast, *el desayuno* (day-sai-OON-oh), usually consists of little more than a white bread roll with white cheese, juice, and coffee, although they may occasionally add an egg. Family members often just eat a quick meal by themselves.

The midday meal, *el almuerzo* (ahl-moo-AIR-soh), is the largest meal of the day and includes at least three courses. The meal begins with a soup (or, in the Costa, with a seafood appetizer called *ceviche*), followed by the main dish, which is accompanied by plenty of rice or potatoes. The main dish may be a thick stew or a fish or chicken dish. The almuerzo sometimes includes a light salad or a side dish of boiled broad beans or other vegetables. The meal concludes with the *postre* (POHS-tray), or dessert, which usually is a serving of fruit, flan (caramel custard), or sweetened, fried plantains.

The family usually sits down to the evening meal, called *cena* (SAY-nah), together. Because Ecuadorians usually work into the evening, the cena tends to be light and may consist of no more than grilled cheese sandwiches or flour or corn pancakes. Or they may have a simpler version of the midday meal, eating meat and rice or potatoes, followed by a light postre.

Ceviche

REGIONAL SPECIALTIES

As in other countries, there are many regional variations in Ecuadorian food. These variations run the gamut from more tropical fare like coconut milk and fish to diets based mostly on grains. Regional cuisines show the diversity of Ecuador's geography. These variations also give a taste of the lifestyles of Ecuadorians around the country.

THE SIERRA Serranos in Ecuador eat a lot of soups and stews made with barley, corn, potatoes, beans, peas, broad beans, squash, quinoa, and melloco (a tuber). Corn in Ecuador is usually served on the cob. The cook may also boil the kernels, parch them, or pop them. Popcorn has been popular for centuries in Ecuador.

Fresh air markets sell *mellocos* by the pound or by the bushel.

Soups are generally known as *caldos* or *sopas*, while the thicker stews are known as *secas* (say-kahs), meaning "dry." People in the Sierra eat soup every day, and the variations are endless. *Locro* (LOH-croh), a "wet" soup, is a traditional Ecuadorian soup made from cheese and potatoes. A fancier version, very popular in the countryside, is made with the heart, liver, and stomach of a cow, sheep, or pig. *Sancocho* (sahn-COH-choh) is another traditional Ecuadorian stew made with plantains and choclos seasoned with cilantro.

Many highland campesinos, on the other hand, survive on little more than barley, either heavily toasted and made into flour or lightly toasted and coarsely ground into barley rice. Many eat barley gruel day after day, occasionally flavored with a lump of fat, a bit of sugar or salt, or a piece of onion or potato. When edible weeds are in season, they stew them with the grain. Fava beans are another main meal. In other areas of the Sierra, quinoa serves the same role. Quinoa is native to the Andes and was considered by the Incas to be a sacred grain.

THE COSTA The Costeño diet consists primarily of coconut milk, peanuts, plantains, noodles, rice, and a lot of seafood and shellfish, including sea bass, shrimp, crab, lobster, and oysters. One of the most popular ways of eating shellfish is in ceviche. In ceviche, the cook does not actually cook the shellfish;

BANANAS

As a major exporter of bananas, Ecuador enjoys a wide variety of bananas and plantains. Several types of bananas and plantains are grown in the Costa and in the Oriente, including tiny finger bananas, or oritas *(oh-REE-tahs); yellow eating bananas; short, fat, red eating bananas, or* magueños *(mah-GAY-nyohs); and large, green cooking plantains. The plantains are used in different ways, depending on their degree of maturity. They are referred to as* verde *(BAYR-day) if green and unripe or* maduro *(mah-DOO-roh) if ripe with a blackened yellow skin. People all over the country eat the starchy fruit in a variety of ways, but they are most popular when deep fried.* Chifles *(CHEE-flais) are a favorite snack,*

made from deep-fried green plantains that have been peeled and thinly sliced into chips. Ecuadorians eat them with the same gusto that North Americans apply to potato chips.

rather, he or she marinates it with onions in lemon or lime juice. Another popular way to prepare fresh fish is to cook it in coconut milk.

Families that depend on wage labor usually eat a poor diet. Rather than rice and beans, as in Central America, poor Costeños subsist on little more than boiled plantains, noodles, and broth. They eat few greens and little protein. Eggs and meat are luxuries.

THE ORIENTE Oriente cuisine is very similar to that of the Costa but includes more game and river fish such as piranha and catfish instead of seafood. The Natives of the Oriente subsist primarily on manioc, a starch, accompanied by peanuts, fish, game, and even certain grubs, which are

Outside of Ecuador, manioc is called cassava or yucca.

eaten either alive or toasted. While such fare as beetle larvae is relatively uncommon in Westernized countries, it is a valuable source of protein in Ecuador.

As in the Costa, plantains are commonly eaten. One popular way of preparing them is to boil and mash them into a drink called *chucula* (choo-KOO-lah), similar to a banana milkshake. When entertaining visitors, the Quechua-speaking Natives also use plantains to make a spicy stew with catfish or game such as the large rodent known as a paca. The Waorani do not hunt large animals such as deer because they believe that these animals are spirits of their ancestors.

BEVERAGES

Tap water in Ecuador is not safe to drink, so many people drink carbonated mineral water, soft drinks, or juice. The variety of fruit juices in Ecuador is mind-boggling. People make them fresh for breakfast, drinking a different kind every morning. The most common types of juice are blackberry, orange, grapefruit, pineapple, passion fruit, guanabana, melon, watermelon, papaya, and naranjilla, which tastes like a bitter orange.

Ecuadorians prepare their coffee by boiling it for hours, until it is reduced to a thick syrup. They store it in a small glass bottle on the table; when they want a cup of coffee, they pour a small amount of the coffee syrup into a cup and fill it up the rest of the way with hot milk or water. Instant coffee has become more popular.

The most common type of alcoholic drink, *aguardiente* (ah-gwa-ar-dee-AIN-tay), or "fire-water," is made from sugarcane alcohol. Rum and beer are

In spite of the fact that Ecuadorian food usually lacks the fire of Peruvian cuisine, hot sauce is always available to kick things up a notch. Aji, Ecuadorian hot sauce made from peppers and garlic, is practically a staple food. It's rare to see a meal served without aji. Recipes vary wildly (there are two varieties of aji—one features tree tomatoes and is yellow in color), but all include onion and cilantro or parsley.

Other Ecuadorian sauces use more mild peppers. It's not unusual to see food served with salsas that range from a slight kick to four alarms. Not all sauces in Ecuador pack spice, though. A peanut sauce called salsa de mani *is served over potatoes, and many traditional sauces have a mayonnaise base.*

also very popular. During fiestas and the Christmas season, people make a sort of hot toddy from aguardiente and cinnamon, with a touch of lemon.

Many indigenous people make a traditional, mildly alcoholic drink called *chicha* (CHEE-cha) by mixing freshly ground corn with boiling water and allowing the mixture to ferment. The people of the Oriente make a thick, slightly alcoholic mash drink as well, which the Waorani call *tepae*. Manioc tepae is the staple food for the Waorani. The women break up the cooked tubers with their fingers, put some into their mouth, chew it, and then spit it back into the pot. It is then allowed to ferment for forty-eight hours. The resulting flavor and consistency is similar to buttermilk, with a slightly alcoholic zest.

COOKING AT HOME

In middle- and upper-class homes, a maid is often responsible for much of the cooking day to day. Kitchens in urban homes contain a refrigerator and a gas or electric range and oven. However, in many homes with refrigerators, Ecuadorians do not bother to refrigerate such foods as cheese, meat, and milk. Automatic dishwashers are not very common because many families employ a domestic worker to do the dishes. (The same is true for automatic washing machines.)

In urban areas, moreover, the municipal supply of running water is often unreliable or scarce, even in homes equipped with water pipes. Thus, Ecuadorians conserve their water carefully when washing the dishes or clothes. They also tend to use cold water for these purposes. Many poor rural and urban homes lack electricity and running water. Indigenous people usually cook over open fires, while sitting or crouching on the ground. Missionaries have tried to introduce the raised platform ovens that many campesinos use, but with little success.

The Otavalo Market includes produce of all varieties.

BUYING GROCERIES

Wealth and customs determine how Ecuadorians shop. The urban middle class and elite shop at supermarkets with canned foods, fresh produce, packaged meat, and household goods, although these cost more than in the United States. Most large towns and cities also have permanent covered markets where many vendors gather to sell their wares. These are generally cheaper than supermarkets but require the buyer to move from vendor to vendor collecting their selections in a bag or basket that they bring themselves. Economic circumstances have forced some middle-class Ecuadorians to seek cheaper alternatives in the covered markets.

In rural towns, there are weekly produce markets where farmers come from the countryside with crops or livestock that they wish to sell. Open-air markets are organized so that meat sellers gather in one area, vegetable sellers in another; vendors selling household goods or crafts likewise have their area or a part of the street if the market spills beyond the town square. Those selling livestock meet where the animals can be tethered for the day. Just about everything is for sale at these markets, including basic medicines, tools, and cleaning products.

INTERNET LINKS

www.thedailymeal.com/best-recipes/ecuadorian
The Daily Meal features a roundup of favorite dishes on the "Best Ecuadorian Recipes" page.

www.nytimes.com/2008/08/17/travel/17journeys.html?_r=0
The *New York Times* takes a closer look at the Ecuadorian street food scene in "Meals and Wheels on Avenue of the Volcanoes."

www.southamerica.cl/ecuador-guide/typical-food.htm
South America Travel Guide provides descriptions of traditional Ecuadorian fare in easy-to-navigate categories like "Appetizers and Street Food," "Main Dishes and Typical Meals," and "Typical Drinks and Beverages from Ecuador."

BAKED *MADUROS* (PLANTAINS)

This recipe for a traditional side dish serves two.

2 overripe plantains (look for brown spots on the skin and a slightly mushy consistency)

Aluminum foil

Nonstick spray

Salt to taste

Preheat your oven to 450°F (230°C).

Cover a baking sheet with aluminum foil.

Before removing the peel, roll each plantain on a hard surface to soften.

Peel the skin, and cut the plantains into ¼-inch (0.6 cm) diagonal slices.

Discard the slices from each end.

Spray the slices with nonstick spray and place on baking sheet.

Bake for 5 minutes, then turn the slices.

Bake for an additional 5 minutes or until the plantains are lightly browned and soft.

Salt the baked plantains, and serve with rice and meat.

LOCRO DE PAPA (POTATO SOUP)

This recipe serves four.

1.5 pounds (700 grams) of potatoes (5 medium-sized white or yellow potatoes)

3.5 cups (840 milliliters) water

1 teaspoon (2.5 g) cumin

1 tablespoon (15 mL) olive oil

1 garlic clove

½ cup (120 mL) milk

½ cup (50 g) shredded Monterey Jack cheese

1 large white onion

½ teaspoon (1 g) achiote powder

½ cup (25 g) chopped cilantro leaves

Dice onion into fine pieces and mince the garlic.

Wash and peel potatoes. Slice into ½-inch (1.3 cm) chunks.

Heat oil in a soup pot.

Add onion, garlic, cumin, and achiote.

Cook until onions turn clear.

Add the potatoes and cook for 3 to 5 minutes.

Pour in water and boil until potatoes soften (approximately 25 minutes).

Using a potato masher, mash potato chunks until mostly creamy.

Pour in milk and cook on low heat for 3 to 5 minutes.

Fold in grated Monterey Jack cheese and cilantro leaves.

Serve with a garnish of avocado, cilantro, hot sauce, and extra cheese if desired.

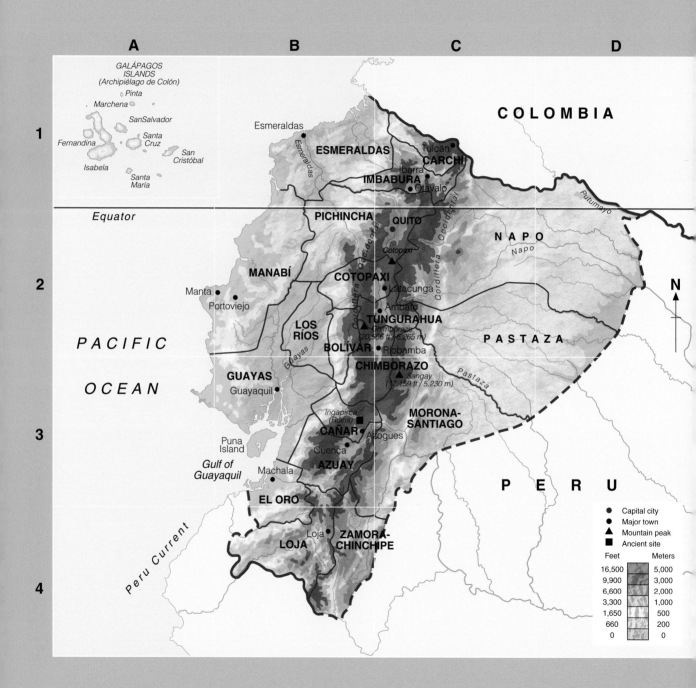

GALÁPAGOS
ISLANDS
(Archipiélago de Colón)

◌ Pinta
● Marchena
● SanSalvador
Santa
Cruz
Fernandina
San
Cristóbal
Isabela
Santa
María

A   **B**   **C**   **D**

COLOMBIA

Esmeraldas

ESMERALDAS

Tulcán ●
CARCHI

Ibarra ●
IMBABURA ●
Otavalo

Equator

PICHINCHA

QUITO ●

NAPO

Cotopaxi ▲

Napo

Putumayo

MANABÍ

COTOPAXI

Latacunga ●

Manta ●
● Portoviejo

Ambato ●
TUNGURAHUA

**LOS
RÍOS**

Chimborazo
(20,556 ft / 6,265 m)

PASTAZA

BOLÍVAR

Riobamba ●

PACIFIC

CHIMBORAZO

Sangay
(17,159 ft / 5,230 m) ▲

OCEAN

GUAYAS

Guayaquil ●

Pastaza

Guayas

**MORONA-
SANTIAGO**

Ingapirca
(Ruins) ■

Puna
Island

CAÑAR

Azogues ●

Cuenca ●

AZUAY

*Gulf of
Guayaquil*

Machala ●

PERU

EL ORO

● Capital city
● Major town
▲ Mountain peak
■ Ancient site

Peru Current

Loja ●
**ZAMORA-
CHINCHIPE**

LOJA

Feet		Meters
16,500		5,000
9,900		3,000
6,600		2,000
3,300		1,000
1,650		500
660		200
0		0

N
▲

MAP OF ECUADOR

Ambato, C2
Azogues, B3
Azuay, B3

Bolívar, B2—B3

Cañar, B3—C3
Carchi, C1
Chimborazo
    (mountain), B2
Chimborazo
    (province), B2,
    B3, C2, C3
Colombia, B1—D1,
    D2
Cordillera
    Occidental, B2—
    B3, C1—C3
Cotopaxi
    (mountain), C2
Cotopaxi
    (province), B2,
    C2
Cuenca, B3

El Oro, B3—B4
Equator, A2—D2
Esmeraldas (city),
    B1
Esmeraldas
    (province), B1, C1
Esmeraldas (river),
    B1

Fernandina, A1

Galápagos Islands,
    A1
Guayaquil, B3
Guayas (province),
    A3, B2—B3
Guayas (river),
    B2—B3
Gulf of Guayaquil,
    A3, B3

Ibarra, C1
Imbabura, B1, C1
Ingapirca, B3
Isabela, A1

Latacunga, C2
Loja (city), B4
Loja (province),
    B3—B4
Los Ríos, B2—B3

Machala, B3
Manabí, A2, B1, B2
Manta, B2
Marchena, A1
Morona-Santiago,
    B3, B4, C2, C3

Napo (province),
    C1, C2, D1, D2

Napo (river), C2,
    D2

Otavalo, C1

Pacific Ocean, A1—
    A4, B1, B2
Pastaza (province),
    C2, C3, D2, D3
Pastaza (river), C3
Peru, A4, B3, B4,
    C3, C4, D2—D4
Peru Current, A4
Pichincha, B1, B2,
    C1, C2
Pinta, A1
Portoviejo, B2
Puna Island, B3
Putumayo (river),
    C1, D1, D2

Quito, C2

Riobamba, C2

Sangay (mountain),
    C3
San Cristóbal, A1
San Salvador, A1
Santa Cruz, A1
Santa María, A1

Tulcán, C1
Tungurahua, B2, C2

Zamora-Chinchipe,
    B3, B4, C4

133

ECONOMIC ECUADOR

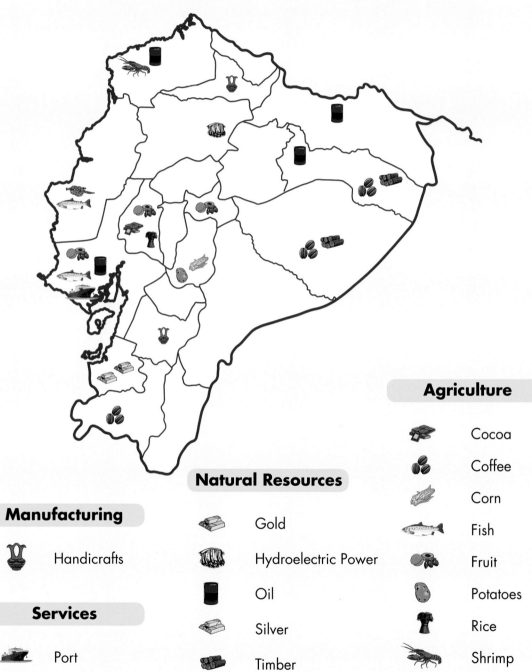

Manufacturing

🏺 Handicrafts

Services

🚢 Port

Natural Resources

Gold

Hydroelectric Power

Oil

Silver

Timber

Agriculture

Cocoa

Coffee

Corn

Fish

Fruit

Potatoes

Rice

Shrimp

ABOUT THE ECONOMY

OVERVIEW
Ecuador has long depended on the success of a single export—from cocoa to bananas to oil. Still heavily dependent on oil exports, Ecuador's economy is vulnerable to fluctuations in global oil prices. The country suffered a major economic crisis in the 1990s after oil prices fell. Higher oil prices since 2003 have helped Ecuador, but the nation has a long way to go in its reforms to reduce its dependence on oil and build its resistance to global price fluctuations.

GROSS DOMESTIC PRODUCT (GDP)
$100.5 billion (2014 estimate)
GDP per capita $11,200 (2014 estimate)

GDP BY SECTOR
Services 59.6 percent, industry 34.4 percent, agriculture 6 percent (2014 estimate)

LAND USE
Forest 38.9 percent, other 31.4 percent, agricultural land 29.7 percent (2011 estimate)

NATURAL RESOURCES
Hydroelectric power, timber, oil, fish

CURRENCY
$1 USD = 100 cents

INFLATION RATE
3.6 percent (2014 estimate)

WORKFORCE
7.214 million (2014 estimate)

WORKFORCE BY OCCUPATION
Services 54.4 percent, agriculture 27.8 percent, industry 17.8 percent (2012 estimate)

UNEMPLOYMENT RATE
5 percent (2014 estimate)

INDUSTRIAL PRODUCTS
Oil, chemicals, food products, textiles, wood products

AGRICULTURAL PRODUCTS
Bananas, coffee, cocoa, rice, potatoes, manioc, plantains, sugarcane, balsa wood, cattle, sheep, pigs, fish, shrimp, dairy products

MAIN EXPORTS
Bananas, cut flowers, shrimp, crude oil, fish

MAIN IMPORTS
Refined oil, automobiles, medicinal products, telecommunications equipment, electricity

TRADE PARTNERS
United States, Peru, Panama, China, Colombia, Venezuela, Brazil, Germany, Chile, Japan

PORTS AND HARBORS
Esmeraldas, Guayaquil, La Libertad, Manta, Puerto Bolivar, San Lorenzo

CULTURAL ECUADOR

Marimba Festival
San Lorenzo comes alive with Afro-Ecuadorian music during the Marimba Festival in May.

Indigenous Culture
Otavalo is the heart of Otavaleño culture, complete with a weekly artisan market and lots of live music in the evenings. In June Otavaleños celebrate the Incan festival of the summer solstice called Inti Raymi.

Mama Negra
In November men dress as women in Latacunga to celebrate the Festival of Mama Negra.

Nature Hot Spot
Mindo is an ecotourist's haven, offering good opportunities for birding, hiking, and rafting.

World Heritage Site
The historical center of Quito is full of colonial architecture and cobblestone roads and was declared a UNESCO World Heritage Site in 1978.

Carnival
Ambato has one of Ecuador's largest Carnival celebrations, with huge parades, including the Festival of Fruit and Flowers.

Ingapirca
Ruins of an Incan city

Music Capital
Loja is home to a musical academy and the country's best musicians. Live entertainment is a nightly affair in the city.

Arts Center
Cuenca, center of the arts in Ecuador, is especially well known for its colonial architecture.

Sangay National Park
This national park, with its incredible natural diversity and beauty, is a World Heritage Site.

COUNTRY NAME
Republic of Ecuador

FLAG DESCRIPTION
Three horizontal bands of yellow (top, double width), blue, and red with the coat of arms superimposed in the center of the flag

NATIONAL ANTHEM
"Salve, Oh Patria" ("We Salute You, Our Homeland")

GOVERNMENT TYPE
Republic

CAPITAL
Quito

ADMINISTRATIVE DIVISIONS
Azuay, Bolívar, Cañar, Carchi, Chimborazo, Cotopaxi, El Oro, Esmeraldas, Galápagos, Guayas, Imbabura, Loja, Los Ríos, Manabí, Morona-Santiago, Napo, Orellana, Pastaza, Pichincha, Santa Elena, Santo Domingo de los Tsáchilas, Sucumbíos, Tungurahua, Zamora-Chinchipe

LAND AREA
106,889 square miles (276,841 square km)

POPULATION
15,868,396 (2015)

LIFE EXPECTANCY
76.56 years, men 73.6 years, women 79.67 years

ETHNIC GROUPS
Montubio 7.4 percent, Amerindian 7 percent, other 6.6 percent, white 6.1 percent, black 1 percent. Though not an ethnic group, mestizos (mixed Amerindian and white) make up 71.9 percent of the population. (2010)

RELIGIONS
Roman Catholic 74 percent, Evangelical 10.4 percent, other (including Protestant and indigenous religions) 15.6 percent

LANGUAGES
Spanish (official), indigenous languages (especially Quechua)

LITERACY RATE
94.5 percent

LEADERS IN POLITICS
Gabriel García Moreno (1861—1875), José Eloy Alfaro Delgado (1895—1901; 1906—1911), José María Velasco Ibarra (sporadically, 1934—1972)

LEADERS IN THE ARTS
Oswaldo Guayasamín (painter), Jorge Icaza (writer), Hugo Cifuentes (photographer), Eugenia Viteri (writer), Gonzalo Endara Crow (painter), Alicia Yanez Cossio (writer)

TIMELINE

IN ECUADOR	IN THE WORLD
4800–1200 BCE Valdivia culture flourishes.	
	753 BCE Rome is founded.
500 BCE–200 CE La Tolita culture flourishes.	
	116–117 CE The Roman Empire reaches its greatest extent.
	600 CE Height of Mayan civilization.
	1000 The Chinese perfect gunpowder and begin to use it in warfare.
1450s Incas arrive from Peru.	
1531 Spaniards land on the Ecuadorian coast and begin their conquest of the Incas.	**1530** Beginning of transatlantic slave trade organized by the Portuguese in Africa.
1534 Spaniards found Quito as a colonial city.	
1645 Epidemics and earthquakes kill thousands in Quito.	**1558–1603** Reign of Elizabeth I of England.
	1776 US Declaration of Independence.
1809 Quiteños begin to push for independence.	**1789–1799** The French Revolution.
1822 Battle of Pichincha; Ecuador becomes part of Gran Colombia.	
1830 Ecuador leaves Gran Colombia and becomes fully independent.	
	1861 The US Civil War begins.
	1869 The Suez Canal is opened.
	1914 World War I begins.
	1939–1945 World War II.
1942 Ecuador cedes part of disputed territory to Peru under the terms of the Rio Protocol.	
1948–1960 Growth in banana trade brings prosperity.	**1949** NATO forms.

IN ECUADOR	IN THE WORLD
	1957
1963	The Russians launch *Sputnik 1*.
Military junta deposes President Carlos Arosemena Monroy.	**1966–1969**
	The Chinese Cultural Revolution.
1967	
Oil is discovered in the Oriente.	
1970	
José María Velasco assumes dictatorial power.	
1972	
Oil production begins; Velasco is overthrown.	**1986**
	Nuclear power disaster at Chernobyl in Ukraine.
	1991
1992	Breakup of the Soviet Union.
Indigenous peoples gain title to Amazonian land.	**1997**
	Hong Kong is returned to China.
2000	
Ecuador adopts the US dollar.	
2001	**2001**
Oil spill threatens the Galápagos Islands.	Terrorists crash planes in New York, Washington, DC, and Pennsylvania.
	2003
	War in Iraq.
2005	**2005**
President Gutierrez is removed from office.	London hit by terrorist bombings.
2006	
Rafael Correa is elected president.	**2008**
	Barack Obama elected US president.
	2011
	"Arab Spring" movement.
2013	**2013**
President Correa is reelected.	Nelson Mandela dies.
2014	**2014**
Rafael Correa's proposal to end presidential term limits is approved by Ecuador's constitutional courts.	ISIS terrorists take over large parts of Syria and Iraq.

GLOSSARY

compadre (kom-PAHD-ray)
Godparent.

cordillera (kor-dee-YAY-rah)
Mountain chain.

Costa
The coastal region.

Costeño
An inhabitant of the Costa, or coastal region.

El Niño
A climatological phenomenon that occurs every six to seven years and causes storms, floods, and landslides.

galápago (gal-AH-pah-goh)
Tortoise.

hacienda (ah-see-EHN-dah)
A large estate, usually in the Sierra.

indigenismo
A school of painting that is defined by its subject—the oppression of indigenous Ecuadorians.

mestizo (mais-TEE-soh)
A person of mixed white and indigenous ancestry.

montuvio (mohn-TOO-vyo)
A person of mixed black, Hispanic, and indigenous ancestry.

Oriente
The eastern, Amazon region.

páramo (PAHR-ah-moh)
Highland area above 11,500 feet (3,500 m).

Quechua
An indigenous language used in Ecuador's Sierra and Oriente regions and other parts of Andean South America. The Incas made Quechua their official language since it was already widely used in the lands they ruled.

Serrano
An inhabitant of the Sierra.

Sierra
The central, mountain region.

torero
Bullfighter.

FOR FURTHER INFORMATION

BOOKS

De La Torre, Carlos, and Steve Striffler, eds. *The Ecuador Reader: History, Culture, Politics.* Durham, NC: Duke University Press, 2009.

Lauderbaugh, George. *The History of Ecuador.* Santa Barbara, CA: Greenwood, 2012.

Nicholls, Henry. *The Galápagos: A Natural History.* New York: Basic Books, 2014.

Westwood, Ben. *Ecuador & the Galápagos Islands.* 5th ed. Berkeley, CA: Avalon Travel, 2012.

WEBSITES

CIA World Factbook. https://www.cia.gov/library/publications/the-world-factbook/geos/ec.html

Ecuador News. http://www.telegraph.co.uk/news/worldnews/southamerica/ecuador

Ecuador Tourism. http://ecuador.travel

Embassy of Ecuador in Washington, DC. http://www.ecuador.org/nuevosite/index_e.php

Unicef Statistics, Ecuador. http://www.unicef.org/infobycountry/ecuador_statistics.html

MUSIC

Cultural Legacy: Traditional Music from Ecuador & Bolivia. Condor Records, 2009.

Ecuador. Cook Records, 2012.

Music of the Jivaro of Ecuador. Folkways Records, 2012.

BIBLIOGRAPHY

BBC News, Ecuador Timeline
http://news.bbc.co.uk/2/hi/americas/country_profiles/1212826.stm.
CIA World Factbook, South America: Ecuador
https://www.cia.gov/library/publications/the-world-factbook/geos/ec.html.
Ecuador.com, Ecuador Channel
http://www.ecuador.com.
"Ecuador President Rafael Correa 'Wins Referendum.'" BBC News. May 8, 2011.
http://www.bbc.com/news/world-latin-america-13325112.
GlobalEDGE, Ecuador: Government
http://globaledge.msu.edu/countries/ecuador/government.
Ministry of Tourism, Ecuador Travel
http://ecuador.travel.
Mino, Maria Dolores. "The Basic Structure of the Ecuadorian Legal System and Legal Research."
NYU Law Global. May 1, 2015.
http://www.nyulawglobal.org/globalex/Ecuador1.html.
Pujol, Layla. "Ecuadorian Sauces." Laylita's Recipes.
http://laylita.com/recipes/ecuadorian-sauces.
Rosenfeld, Everett. "Let's Get Digital! Ecuador's New Currency." CNBC. February 9, 2015.
http://www.cnbc.com/2015/02/06/ecuador-becomes-the-first-country-to-roll-out-its-own-digital-durrency.html.
UNdata, Ecuador
http://data.un.org/CountryProfile.aspx?crName=ECUADOR.

INDEX

INDEX